Travis Swann Taylor

111 Places
in Phoenix
That You Must
Not Miss

T0243802

emons:

Bibliographical information of the Deutsche Nationalbibliothek
The Deutsche Nationalbibliothek lists this publication in
the Deutsche Nationalbibliografie; detailed bibliographical data
are available on the internet at http://dnb.d-nb.de.

© Emons Verlag GmbH
All rights reserved
© Photographs by Travis Swann Taylor, except see p. 238
© Cover icon: Shutterstock/Bernadette Heath; Shutterstock/Mr Doomits
Coverdesign: Karolin Meinert
Layout: Eva Kraskes, based on a design
by Lübbeke | Naumann | Thoben
Maps: altancicek.design, www.altancicek.de
Basic cartographical information from Openstreetmap,
© OpenStreetMap-Mitwirkende, OdbL
Edited by: Karen E. Seiger
Printing and binding: Grafisches Centrum Cuno, Calbe
Printed in Germany 2024
ISBN 978-3-7408-2050-3
First edition

Guidebooks for Locals & Experienced Travelers
Join us in uncovering new places around the world at
www.111places.com

Foreword

This book represents the beginning of a relationship fueled, in part, by a love of wanderlust, a desire to experience new places, and tastebuds eager to discover fresh and unique flavors. Rob and I met in Georgia, where he was born and where I lived for 26 years. But he has lived in Phoenix for more than 30 years. His knowledge of the city gave me an exceptional head start on getting to know it myself.

That beginning has led us to one adventure after another. My first week in Phoenix, just before making the Sonoran Desert my new home, took us to the Desert Botanical Garden to see a rare crested saguaro. We toured downtown, where we got to engage with Doug Boyd's *Bernie the Robot*, a work of art that encourages us all to look up from our smartphones. And we discovered some creative flavors at LIX Uptown Ice Cream.

I love connecting the dots. I learned that the 1948 Encanto Carousel was saved by locals and that artist Maggie Keane, the artist behind the *Prince Tribute Mural*, had restored and repainted the carousel horses. Learning from Rob about *The Family Circus* cartoonist's final resting place took me to McCormick-Stillman Railroad Park, where Arizona's "Merci Train" is on display. Looking for the best tacos took us to Grand Avenue, where we discovered the former Bragg's Pie Factory, which used to bake nearly 20,000 pies daily! One of the businesses in the building today is Bacanora, where Executive Chef Rene Andrade won a James Beard Best Chef Award.

Rob helped with exploring potential sites, and his involvement ignited for him a renewed love of photography. He loves taking photos of Phoenix, including some of the ones on these pages.

This book is a gift to local Phoenicians and visitors alike to instill a newfound, unquenchable thirst for exploring and discovering places across the Valley of the Sun. Enjoy wandering all over our wonderful hometown of Phoenix.

111 Places

1 __ 9/11 Memorial Pony

World's largest firefighting museum

Walking up to the Hall of Flame Firefighting Museum, you can't imagine what you're about to experience. This "hall" is massive. It's mesmerizing. And it chronicles the heroism and lives of those protecting our citizens from life-threatening fires. The collection, with its origins in Wisconsin, is very exciting. The oldest fire engine here was made in England in 1725, or seven years before the first US President George Washington was even born. There are six major galleries, with more than 130 wheeled pieces and over 10,000 other artifacts.

The 9/11 Memorial Pony is featured in the Hall of Heroes Gallery. This beautiful yet solemn tribute, a life-sized statue of the American Quarter Horse, is dedicated to the 343 firefighters, 23 NYPD, and the 37 NY and NJ Port Authority officers who lost their lives the day the World Trade Center towers were attacked, while helping more than 25,000 civilians escape. This horse was the 120th in the previously 119-piece collection of the "Painted Ponies" public art exhibition hosted in Santa Fe, New Mexico. Its custom paint ranges from fire engine red, to flame yellow with hues of a deep metallic pink, to a brilliant copper. The boots in the stirrups are placed backward, symbolizing the death of a great person. The horse is standing with dignity on a "coffin" containing a NYFD helmet, a NYPD cap, and a NY/NJ Port Authority cap.

In Gallery III is fire engine NYFD Rescue 4, which is one of the vehicles that responded to the attack on the World Trade Center towers in 2001. The eight fire fighters who rode this truck to the site perished in the line of duty that day.

The museum offers a wide variety of exhibits, including fire apparatus, artwork, uniforms and equipment, firemarks, firehouse uniform patches, alarm room equipment, a mini theater, and many hands-on exhibits and photo-ops for grownups and future first responders.

Address 6101 E Van Buren Street, Phoenix, AZ 85005, +1 (602) 275-3473, www.hallofflame.org, info@hallofflame.org | Getting there Valley Metro Light Rail to Priest Drive/Washington Street | Hours Tue–Sat 10am–6pm | Tip Since 1902, more than 150 firefighters and paramedics have lost their lives protecting Metro Phoenix citizens. The Arizona Firefighters & Emergency Paramedics Memorial was completed in 2016 at Wesley Bolin Memorial Plaza, beautifully capturing their service in numerous sculptures (1700 W Washington Street, www.azfirefightersmemorial.com).

2 Airport Art Collection

A phoenix, giant aviators, and so much more

Featuring one of the largest and oldest airport art programs in the world, Phoenix Sky Harbor International Airport (PHX) is home to more than 1,000 pieces in its permanent collection, considerably more than can be displayed at any one time but ample for their changing exhibition program. The collection primarily focuses on works by Arizona artists.

The gallery in Terminal 4, Level 3, typically features new acquisitions, usually of a variety of artistic mediums, and it's a great place to start your airport art walk through the publicly accessible areas. You will find art in Terminal 4, Terminal 3, an outdoor sculpture garden, and the Rental Car Center, and many of the architectural elements that are literally works of art themselves.

Exploring the art in America's Friendliest Airport® serendipitously includes an airport history lesson, in addition to the Phoenix aviation history displays. The City of Phoenix purchased the then budding airport in 1935. Terminal 2 was built with art in mind. Its iconic Phoenix mural by the late Paul Coze (1903 – 1974) depicts the city's past, present, and future at the time, and it's spectacular. When Terminal 2 was closed in 2020 after 58 years, including a renovation in 2007 that masked some of the Brutalist aesthetic, the Coze mural was saved and relocated to the Rental Car Center in 2021. Terminal 3 is home to Donald Lipski's *The Aviators* (2018) – the iconic sunglasses even have functional arms. Terminal 4, the largest space at PHX, has art practically everywhere.

Many of the artworks have a QR Code, giving travelers and visitors alike access to information about specific pieces in the airport's collection. There are also paper postcards at points throughout the airport that feature some of the artworks, and they're free. Share your modern airport art experience old school-style and snail-mail a postcard to family or a friend.

Address 3400 Sky Harbor Boulevard, Phoenix, AZ 85034, www.skyharbor.com/at-the-airport/amenities/airport-museum | Getting there Valley Metro Light Rail to 44th Street/Washington, then PHX Skytrain to Terminal 4 | Hours Unrestricted | Tip Why would you jump out of a perfectly good airplane? Because it's so much fun. Head to Skydive Phoenix for the experience of a lifetime, with spectacular views (56580 W Dasher Drive, Maricopa, www.skydivephoenix.com).

3 Alwun House

Downtown art pioneers, of a unique sort

Alwun House has the distinction of being the first art gallery in downtown Phoenix, still today honoring its roots as a home to alternative, contemporary, and exploratory arts in the form of gallery showings and signature events showcasing performance art. When it was built in 1912, the same year that Arizona was granted statehood, the house sat on five acres in the middle of nowhere, and was architecturally unique. Its design was inspired by the bungalow style, with some detailing whispering of the colonial or mission styles. Its sheer size – two stories and a basement – and its lush landscaping, including tall trees, make it a standout in the Garfield Historic District.

With a single glance, you will know you're at the right place because you can't miss the bright, bold colors of this corner lot, historic home, or, from time to time, the sculptural elements gracing the front yard. Those might range from a giant spider over the entry walkway during Halloween season, to a door-sized, steampunk watch dial. Whatever the piece may be, it's a nod to the current art exhibition. "Exotic Show," their signature event featuring multiple artists, blurs the lines between exotic and erotic for some people. The performance art not only bumps up against edgy, but it also draws excited crowds. What the city would call "artistic events and gatherings" are some of the most fun nights out that Phoenix's alternative scene has to offer, throughout the year.

If you're wondering about the name Alwun, it's a portmanteau for "All arts in one place" and pronounced "all-one." Alwun House Foundation is brilliant at integrating arts of various media and presenting them together, or all one. When you visit, don't be surprised if you see a very friendly Great Dane, the canine companion of gallery owners Kim Moody, one of the founders, and his partner Dana Johnson.

Address 1204 E Roosevelt Street, Phoenix, AZ 85006, +1 (602) 253-7887, www.alwunhouse.org, alwun@AlwunHouse.org | Getting there Bus 10 to Roosevelt & 12th Streets | Hours Tue–Fri noon–6pm | Tip Nearby and still in the Historic Garfield Neighborhood is Joe Tyler's *Garfield Rising*, an 18-foot-tall, steel sculpture depicting a phoenix rising from dramatic flames (E Roosevelt & 13th Streets, www.garfieldneighborhood.org/loc/20211002-garfield-rising).

4 Anthem Veterans Memorial
Solar spotlight at 11:11am on 11/11

Five white-marble pillars standing upon red-brick pavers under the blue Arizona sky – these elements representing the colors of the American flag are the primary components of the unique Anthem Veterans Memorial, a solemn place of honor to reflect on the sacrifices made by the men, women, and families in the Armed Forces. Every Veterans Day on November 11 at 11:11am, the sun's rays pass through the five ellipses of the Memorial's pillars to cast a solar spotlight on a hand-cut-glass mosaic of the Great Seal of the United States.

All of the elements of the memorial are symbolic in some fashion. The five pillars represent the five branches of the military. They are staggered in size, ranging in height from 6 to 17 feet tall, and on each pillar's two sides are their appropriate military seals in stainless steel. The pillars are arranged in the Department of Defense Order of Precedence. The Circle of Honor, composed of more than 2,000 red-brick pavers engraved with names of veterans, represents solidarity among the US Armed Forces. There are five benches around the Circle of Honor that symbolize the families of service members from each military branch, who also make sacrifices, especially while waiting for their loved ones to return home. On the other side of the glass-mosaic seal is a flag pole flying the American flag and the National League of Families POW/MIA flag.

This memorial, designed by renowned artist Renee Palmer-Jones, was dedicated on Veterans Day 2011. Annual public ceremonies are held at the Memorial every Memorial Day and Veterans Day to commemorate veterans who died while serving their country and those who are missing in action.

Anthem Community Park, where the Memorial is located, also features baseball fields and basketball and pickleball courts, an amusement park, playgrounds, a little train ride for the kiddos, multiple lakes, and walking trails.

Address 41703 N Gavilan Peak Parkway, Anthem, AZ 85086, www.onlineatanthem.com/
visitors/veterans_memorial/index.php | Getting there By car, take I-17 N to exit 229, and
turn east onto W Anthem Way and then right onto N Gavilan Peak Parkway | Hours
Daily 6am–10pm | Tip Directly west, Lake Pleasant, billed as a "recreationist's dream,"
offers camping, boating, fishing, swimming, hiking, picnicking, and wildlife viewing
(41835 N Castle Hot Springs Road, Morristown, www.maricopacountyparks.net/park-
locator/lake-pleasant-regional-park).

5 Arizona Doll & Toy Museum

A 300-year-old doll and Mr. Spock, too

The Arizona Doll & Toy Museum may look modest on the outside, but on the inside it's home to a collection that is as fascinating as it is extensive. Their primary focus is on vintage dolls, but they are growing the toy collection. The earliest known dolls – cited as the earliest playthings – date back 3,000 years, some found in Egyptian graves. The oldest doll in this collection, wearing a yellow dress, is around 300 years old. A few more contemporary, recognizable dolls include Howdy Doody, Shirley Temple, G. I. Joe, Barbie, American Girl, Betty Boop, R2-D2 and C-3PO, and Mr. Spock.

In the early 1400s there were Dochenmacher, or doll makers, in Nürnberg, Germany, which, from the 16th to the 18th century, was the leading manufacturer of dolls. Paris was another early mass-producer of dolls. Dollhouses – the museum has several spectacular examples – have been popular in Europe since the 16th century. Time permitting, extremely knowledgeable Kathy Lanford, Museum Curator & Director, may point out some highlights within the museum's doll population – she is a doll collector herself and had worked at the museum before it moved to historic Catlin Court in Glendale from Heritage Square in downtown Phoenix. Founded in 1988, today the museum features dolls of all shapes and sizes, from different generations and countries. The styles of dolls and toys range from China to bisque, tin to paper, and plastic to wax.

The museum also has at least two Charlie McCarthy dolls. This ventriloquist's counterpart made his stage debut in 1922. His human was Edgar Bergan, an Oscar-winner and USO entertainer. Dioramas include highly detailed millinery and tailor shops, as well as an ice cream and soda fountain shoppe. Perhaps the most popular attraction here is the 1912 schoolroom with a class full of student dolls.

Address 5847 W Myrtle Avenue, Glendale, AZ 85301, +1 (623) 939-6186, www.azdollandtoymuseum.com | **Getting there** Bus 59, GAL to 59th & Myrtle Avenues | **Hours** Wed–Sat 10am–4pm | **Tip** Dobson Ranch Park offers a massive 10,000-square-foot playground for children of all abilities to enjoy, with shaded picnic facilities for the whole family to enjoy (2359 S Dobson Road, Mesa, www.mesaparks.com/parks-facilities/parks/dobson-ranch-park).

6 — Arizona Falls
Phoenix's first hydroelectric power plant

Thousands of people drive by Arizona Falls every day, unaware of the significance of this unique site. The 20-foot waterfall here is actually part of an engineering marvel and a wholly pleasant experience to visit.

Around 1,500 years ago, the Hohokam Indians built canals from the Salt River to irrigate the valley to grow crops. Fast-forward to 1867, when the earliest settlers of Phoenix resurrected and added to that canal system, also to irrigate crops for what would become the country's fifth largest city and one of its largest metro areas. In 1902, engineers constructed Phoenix's first hydroelectric power plant between today's 56th and 58th Streets. In 1911, the Salt River Project (SRP) reconstructed the generators – adding a powerhouse that covered the falls – that would remain in operation until 1950.

In 1998, a modern Arizona Falls was in its infancy. The idea for a sustainable power generation demonstration site was the catalyst that fueled the project, and a design firm was selected in 2000. The former powerhouse was demolished in 2002, and Arizona Falls is once again a gathering place for the community and visitors from around the world. The onsite boulders are from SRP dams. Thought-provoking phrases etched on the upper platform include, "Because water reflects, it holds everything." The lower viewing platform places visitors between three sheets of waterfalls, a unique experience in Phoenix. The fish here are a sustainable solution for algae that typically grows at such sites.

Arizona Falls' tiny footprint generates enough electricity to power 150 homes. Its onsite ceiling fans, powered by solar panels, and shade structures make for a pleasant visit year-round. The main entrance is on the canal's south side, and there's a footbridge connecting walkers, runners, and cyclists to the viewing platform of this historic neighborhood gem.

Address 5802 E Indian School Road, Phoenix, AZ 85018, www.srpnet.com/grid-water-management/water-recreation/canal-trails/arizona-falls | **Getting there** Bus 41 to Indian School Road & 56th Street | **Hours** Unrestricted | **Tip** Meet up with friends at the Arizona Canal South Bridge in Old Town Scottsdale and explore the ancient-modern canal system of Phoenix, today peppered with art, shops, bites, and drinks. It's one of the best places for exercise and sightseeing in town (South Bridge, Scottsdale, www.visitphoenix.com/stories/post/canal-walks).

7 — Arizona Latino Arts & Cultural Center

Raising up Latin American culture

From the street, you see the wonderfully colorful gallery and the art-filled La Tiendita gift shop, but what lies beyond those few front walls will astound you. This space is massive. The Arizona Latino Arts & Cultural Center (ALAC), a nonprofit organization led by executive director and artist Elizabeth Toledo, is a first-of-its-kind in Arizona.

ALAC "serves as a beacon of cultural and artistic expression through art exhibits, film, theater, presentations, lectures, live performances and literary readings," and more, as its website states. Numerous resident artists have their studios here. It also is home to globally available Latino USA TV. Music videos are filmed here, poetry readings are hosted here, and a wide variety of events and classes is offered. It also serves as the steward of and repository for Arizona Barrio Stories, a collection of oral histories.

One of the resident artists, also an ALAC co-founder, is Roman P. Reyes, whose family moved to Phoenix when he was a youngster. He would become a lifelong artist, creating sculptures from clay in the local canals as a kid, and educator. He worked on special effects, masks, bodysuits, and sets for the multiple Academy Award-winning *Lord of the Rings* trilogy. He retired as professor emeritus from Phoenix College, and his work has been displayed in the White House.

In La Tiendita, you will find Reyes' art, as well as that of José Andrés Girón, Carlos L. J. Montufar, and Elizabeth Toledo, among others. Ninety percent of the art in the gift shop has been created by local artists, and the inventory is constantly renewed, especially by the resident artists. This is the perfect downtown destination to find a hyper-local souvenir or gift for a loved one – or a treat for yourself.

Address 147 E Adams Street, Phoenix, AZ 85004, +1 (602) 254-9817, www.alacarizona.org, azlatinoarts@gmail.com | Getting there Valley Metro Light Rail to 3rd Street/Washington | Hours Tue–Sat noon–6pm | Tip Enjoy a flight of tequilas or a specialty mezcal cocktail at Barcoa Agaveria's basement bar (829 N 1st Avenue, www.barcoaphx.com).

8 Base and Meridian Marker

From where (almost) all Arizona land is measured

Nearly all of Arizona, except a portion of the Navajo Reservation in the northeast part of the state, was surveyed from this point. The 150-foot-tall Monument Hill offers an easy ascent to the top and spectacular views. Here, you will find the geological marker known as the "Initial Point," the spot from which all land in Arizona is measured. X marks the spot here, as the east-west portion of the cross-like marker is topped with blue and white tiles and runs parallel with the Gila and Salt Rivers. The north-south portion, pointing to the desert and mountains that flank the region, is topped with orange, yellow, purple, and teal tiles. The property is on the National Register of Historic Places.

To the north, the Gila and Salt River Meridian, named for the confluence of the Gila and Salt Rivers, extends to the horizon as Avondale Boulevard, becoming 115th Avenue in North Metro Phoenix. To the south, the meridian is the boundary between the Gila River Indian Reservation and county park land. To the east, you're seeing the reservation. The baseline is visible on the ground as it becomes the arterial Baseline Road, which stretches well beyond Phoenix. Downtown is in the distance on the left. Turn around and look west towards the Phoenix Raceway.

The first marker here was an eight-foot-tall rock monument placed in 1851 as part of the US/Mexico boundary survey. In 1865, the monument was selected as the initial point for surveys in Arizona. Over a century later in 1984, a re-monumentation and preservation of this historic point became a joint effort undertaken by groups named on metal discs on the monument. Another major restoration took place in 2006. As of 2012, approximately 62 million acres of Arizona land have been surveyed from this point. The remaining 11 million acres is nearly all military reservations, national parks and forest, and Indian reservations.

Address S Avondale Boulevard, south of the Gila River, Avondale, AZ 85353 | Getting there By car, take I-10 to exit 131 to S Avondale Boulevard, and then turn left in front of Phoenix Raceway | Hours Unrestricted | Tip If the racetrack is tempting you, give in to a NASCAR experience at Phoenix Raceway (7602 Jimmie Johnson Drive, Avondale, www.phoenixraceway.com).

9 The Bat Cave
Thousands of bats in dramatic flight

On the north side of the Arizona Canal, near 40th Street and Camelback Road, is a flood control tunnel. It also happens to be a real-life bat cave! Experts estimate that 10,000–20,000 bats visit every year to bear their young and decimate the area's population of mosquitoes and crop pests. You can witness the bats' dramatic flight from an observation deck just above the cave.

Though often misunderstood, bats are crucial for the local ecosystem. Did you know that bats are the only mammal capable of sustained flight? There are 28 species in Arizona, and the local Mexican free-tailed bats are of the smaller variety, with bodies only 2–4 inches long and wingspans of about 12 inches. They're also among the fastest, flying at up to 65 miles per hour while feeding in flight. A single colony can consume tons of insects in a month.

You'll have to find parking and then walk to the fenced-off viewing space. It's a fascinating and fun destination, but it's not a place you just happen upon, unless you jog or walk regularly along the Arizona Canal Trail. Once you arrive, you must wait patiently and quietly. If the bats hear loud noises, they may not emerge from their lair and that means the mommy bats are not out foraging for their newborn baby bats.

The Flood Control District of Maricopa County is the mindful steward of the local maternity colony of bats. The baby bats, or pups, are born May through June and can take up to six weeks before they can fly. But you can see the thousands of mother bats take flight May through October at dusk, just minutes before sunset. According to research, bats use sophisticated sonar communication techniques. According to National Geographic, there's research that male bats' songs contain a set of syllables, differentiating themselves from other bat species, that are intended to attract females. Listen quietly and you just might hear a love song.

Address Northwest of the intersection of N 40th Street & E Camelback Road, on the north side of Arizona Canal, Phoenix, AZ 85018 | **Getting there** By car, take I-10 east to exit 2, turn left and continue on N 40th Street to just north of Camelback Road and over the Arizona Canal, then walk northwest along the Arizona Canal to destination | **Hours** Daily May–Oct at dusk | **Tip** Birdwatching in Phoenix is plentiful, and the variety of birds is astounding. Visit the Nina Mason Pulliam Rio Salado Audubon Center, south of downtown, where you can see more than 200 species (3131 S Central Avenue, riosalado.audubon.org).

10 Battleship Silver Service
Stately tableware shines solemnly

If you've ever been to a fancy dinner party, you may have dined with actual silverware. Or perhaps you've enjoyed a bottle of champagne chilled in a silver wine bucket on a special occasion. Most people have never dined with the likes of a battleship's silver service, though. As tradition holds, the USS *Arizona* was christened on June 19, 1915 by Esther Ross, the 17-year-old daughter of a Prescott, Arizona pioneer. Selected by Arizona Governor W. P. Hunt, Ross ceremoniously smashed a bottle of champagne and a bottle of the first water to flow over Hoover Dam across the bow, though the water bottle did not explode.

Commissioned in 1916, the USS *Arizona* remained Stateside during World War I and later escorted President Woodrow Wilson to the 1919 Paris Peace Conference. The 87-piece, formal silver service was presented to the USS *Arizona*, also in 1919. The silver would not sink with the battleship in Pearl Harbor, as it had been placed in storage in January 1941 with the foresight of impending war. You can see it all today at the Arizona Capitol Museum.

The centerpiece of the collection is a gargantuan punchbowl made of solid silver with certain elements of burnished native copper to showcase Arizona's mineral richness. The collection of pieces is decorated with American flags, American Bald Eagles, saguaro and other cacti, as well as nautical themes. A single item, one of the bread baskets, bears an engraving of the USS *Arizona*. The majestic punch bowl towers on feet of dolphins, and the handles are two mermaids, beautiful creatures of naval folklore.

The silver service would be placed on two other ships before being returned to the State of Arizona. It was on display at the Arizona State Fair for two years and then spent time in a bank. It was moved to the new Capitol Tower, and it has been on view for the public's enjoyment at this museum since 1991.

Address 1700 W Washington Street, Phoenix, AZ 85007, +1 (602) 926-3620, www.azcapitolmuseum.gov, museum@azleg.gov | Getting there Bus 514, 521, 522, 531, 533, 535, 542, 562 to 17th Avenue & State Capitol | Hours Mon–Fri 9am–4pm, Sat 10am–2pm | Tip Enjoy a boat ride at Tempe Town Lake, either on a paddle boat, swan boat, duck boat, or a dragon boat. They also have donut boats for larger groups (72 W Rio Salado Parkway, Tempe, www.boats4rent.com/tempe-az/tempe-town).

11 _Bernie the Robot_

Reminding you to look up from your phone

It was while hiking 130 of California's 211-mile John Muir Trail in the Sierra Nevada mountains, which has the mildest, sunniest climate of any major mountain range in the world, that metal artist Doug Boyd realized something. Even as he walked amidst some of the most beautiful mountains in the world, he was still connected to his phone, using it for GPS and to take photos. So he began wondering, "What if someday we all become so connected to our technology that we evolve into robots? But then, life being a full-circle proposition, those robots eventually rediscover what humans had abandoned, such as nature or even books." This moment was the inspiration for _Bernie the Robot_.

In glorious irony, this sculpted robot is delightfully reading a book, while passing humans are engrossed in their devices, sometimes not even noticing this magnificent work of art. The green streetlight (and solar panel) and the blue bench are part of the sculpture. On the pages of the book in Bernie's hands is the story of how he came to be, how the epiphany of being too connected to technology nearly overpowered the importance of being connected to nature. It's signed, "Doug Boyd, 2019."

The moral to _Bernie the Robot's_ story is that we should all step away from our devices every once in a while to embrace and relish life's simplest pleasures. The planter that he's situated next to shows in large letters the address "111 West Monroe." So some locals have affectionately nicknamed him "Monrobot." When you visit _Bernie the Robot_ during the evening hours, you will see the streetlight, his piercing blue eyes, and his circular, glowing, red heart all illuminated. The vision of Bernie in this lit-up state reminded one fan of the 1982 Neil Diamond song with the refrain, "Turn on your heartlight…Let it shine wherever you go…Let it make a happy glow…For all the world to see…"

Address 111 W Monroe Street, Phoenix, AZ 85004, www.artfullyrogue.com/about |
Getting there Valley Metro Light Rail to Van Buren/1st Avenue or Washington/Central
Avenue; bus 3, 514, 521, 522, 531, 533, 535 to Van Buren Street & 1st Avenue | Hours
Unrestricted | Tip Another book-reader, and another of Doug Boyd's works, the six-foot-
tall *Blue Rhino* sits brilliantly in front of the Peoria Main Library, where he is perusing the
1963 book *Where the Wild Things Are* by Maurice Sendak (8463 W Monroe Street, Peoria,
peoria.polarislibrary.com/polaris).

12 The Bible Museum

Not your standard hotel Bibles

You are not likely to stumble across the Bible Museum, unless perhaps you are a guest at the Hampton Inn & Suites Phoenix-Goodyear. Yes, this museum is inside a suburban hotel with no signage for it outside. But it has the significance of being the world's largest for-sale collection of ancient Bibles and the only full-time professional dealer of rare and antique Bibles with a public showroom. The showroom is modest in size but wholly deserving of a visit.

Open since 1987, the Bible Museum has two large, acrylic-domed display cases with more than a dozen antique Bibles on display. Placards tell the story of each individual Bible on exhibit, and some provide a brief history lesson too. Because all of the Bibles are available for purchase in the museum and online, you'll see different ones whenever you visit. You may find the 1537 Matthew's Bible, the author of which was executed for his efforts – you can bring it home for $300,000. Look for an 1852 first edition, first printing copy of the first Catholic English New Testament. And there's a 1791 Collins Family Bible, an early example of the tradition of having a beautifully bound, highly illustrated Bible in the home, often inscribed with information about births and deaths within the family.

Along the walls are glass-front bookcases housing some of the museum's quite valuable antique Bibles. The museum houses a number of ancient artifacts, too, some on display, some under lock and key. But you can simply ask to see them. Look for the one object that displays cuneiform characters, the earliest known writing system.

If you would like to purchase a souvenir to mark your experience here, there are laminated posters of biblical timelines, genealogy, maps, and more. You can find some of the same items in pamphlet form, as well as some additional reference materials. Book a free private tour for eight or more people.

Address 2000 N Litchfield Road, Goodyear, AZ 85395, +1 (623) 536-8614,
www.thebiblemuseum.com, thebiblemuseumaz@gmail.com | Getting there By car, take
I-10 W to exit 128, turn right onto N Litchfield Road | Hours Unrestricted, tours available |
Tip Only 10 minutes north is the P. W. Litchfield Heritage Center, where you can learn
about the history of the Southwest Valley (13912 W Camelback Road, Litchfield Park,
www.pwlhc.org).

13 Bil Keane's Tomb

A beloved cartoonist depicted family funnies

If you have ever read the funny papers, you likely know *The Family Circus*. It's the comic "strip" that's actually penned in a circle. Bil Keane moved his family to Metro Phoenix in 1959, and the next year he began creating The Family Circus despite having no artistic training. Today, it is the most widely syndicated comic panel in the world, appearing in nearly 1,500 newspapers in print, as well as online. Bil and his wife Thelma, or "Thel," raised their children in a house in Paradise Valley, which they purchased in 1960, the same year Bil started The Family Circus. They lived there until he passed away in 2011.

Their final resting place is in North Phoenix at the Holy Redeemer Catholic Cemetery, a newer cemetery founded in 2000. It is meticulously maintained and beautifully designed with the natural desert environment front of mind. Before you reach the cemetery, you will see a very large, white cross situated at the back of the property. Upon a brilliant green lawn are handsome mausoleums with a cross design on the sides, as well as fountains, a babbling brook, bronze and marble statuary, stained glass, and several themed gardens, one named for Saint John Paul II.

Bil's was the first above-ground tomb here. On the front of the tomb are Bil and Thelma's names, and just above that are the faces of the four cartoon kids: Jeffy, Billy, Dolly, and P. J. At the top it reads, "The Circle of Life Continues Eternally." And inscribed at the bottom, "The Parents of Gayle, Neal, Glen, Chris, Jeff," their actual children. Most of the inscriptions are in the same font used to pen the cartoon. When Bil was still living, his son Jeff began working with his father on the comic, bringing smiles to faces around the world. Jeff would go off to college, get married, and have children of his own, and then return to take up the torch of The Family Circus.

Address 23015 N Cave Creek Road, Phoenix, AZ 85024, +1 (480) 513-3243, www.hrccem.org/locations/holy-redeemer-catholic-cemetery, info@dopccfh.org | **Getting there** By car, take I-10 east to State Route-51 north to Exit 51A to Route 101 west, then take exit 28 and turn right onto Cave Creek Road | **Hours** Gates: daily 8am–6pm | **Tip** Designed by Keane's sons Jeff and Glen, the *Giddy-Up, Daddy* statue features Keane himself giving a horsey ride to his cartoon kids (7301 E Indian Bend Road, Scottsdale, www.therailroadpark.com/familycircuspavilion).

14 Blonde Butcher's House

Where jealousy led to murder

Nestled between what is today's Phoenix Country Club and St. Thomas Hospital on a relatively quiet street is an adorable bungalow where several friends lived together, seemingly in harmony…at least for a while. There were only three people present at the October 1931 homicides, which the press would soon call the "Trunk Murders."

The news outlets also wrote about the "Blonde Butcher," Winnie Ruth Judd (1905 – 1998), a medical secretary at nearby Grunow Memorial Medical Center. She was accused of murdering her friends Agnes Anne LeRoi and Hedvig Samuelson, allegedly to win over the affections of Jack Halloran, a prominent Phoenix businessman. She remained silent at her own trial.

Two days after the murders, Judd had boarded an overnight train to Los Angeles, transporting the bodies in two travel trunks, one black and considerably larger than the other, as Samuelson's body had been dismembered. Three days after Judd's arrival in Los Angeles, a railroad worker reported a "foul odor" coming from the trunks. Police began looking for her, but she surrendered less than a week later at a local funeral home. Already sensationalized in newspapers, Judd was tried and convicted of LeRoi's murder and sentenced to die by hanging. However the verdict was overturned, and she was committed to the Arizona State Asylum for the Insane in 1933. There was only one woman who was ever legally hanged in Arizona, but that's a different story.

Judd escaped numerous times – by some accounts it was six, while others say seven. After one of her escapes, she remained at large for many years. She was eventually paroled and moved to California, but she returned to Phoenix for the final years of her life. She passed away in her sleep at a friend's home. She was 93 years old. The Phoenix Theatre Company hosted the world premiere of the play *The Truth About Winnie Ruth Judd* in 2024.

Address 2947 N 2nd Street, Phoenix, AZ 85012 | Getting there Valley Metro Light Rail to Thomas/Central Avenue; bus 29 to Thomas Road & 3rd Street | Hours Unrestricted from the outside only | Tip Winnie Ruth Judd took her two trunks to Union Station and caught her train to Los Angeles. Built in 1923, the station was in operation until 1996. Events can be held at this beautiful historic site now, and rumors abound about its future (401 W Harrison Street).

15 Bragg's Pie Factory

Now a haven for local artists and entrepreneurs

Still towering over one of the only cast-in-place, International-style buildings remaining in Phoenix, is a sign in a unique font marking the former site of Bragg's Pie Factory. Allan and Elaine Bragg built the complex in 1946–47 to accommodate their expanding pie business, which they had started in 1935. The site facilitated baking and deliveries, and had a retail space on the corner with floor-to-ceiling windows.

By the 1940s, the Bragg's were baking nearly 20,000 pies every day, selling them to restaurants, grocery stores, and locals. The giant sign over the pie factory of yesteryear once bore the name of Goodman's Office Furniture. When the building was purchased in 2004 by Beatrice Moore and Tony Zahn to save it from the wrecking ball, the sign was repainted with "Bragg's Pie Factory" in the font that matched the former storefront sign.

Along the southern stretch of Grand Avenue, which begins at 7th Avenue and Van Buren Street in downtown, are at least 55 large, colorful, concrete planters that contain desert-friendly greenery and are painted with phenomenally clever artwork. The planters alone will make a stroll down Grand Avenue – exploring its art galleries, eateries, watering holes, and small businesses – quite memorable, but there's more. On the stretch of sidewalk of the former factory, the trees are blanketed with colorful, mesmerizing crochet work. Those palms and other trees with significant trunk size are bedazzled with faeries, unicorns, plush toys, ornaments, silk flowers, and any and everything Cyndi Lauper might have worn in the 1980s, in the best of ways.

The building is now on the Phoenix Historic Property Register and the National Register of Historic Places. In the retail space today is Bacanora, a Sonoran cuisine Mexican restaurant, where Executive Chef Rene Andrade won a 2024 James Beard Award for Best Chef – Southwest.

Address 1301 Grand Avenue, Phoenix, AZ 85007, www.grandavenueartsandpreservation.org | Getting there Bus 15 to 15th Avenue & Roosevelt Street | Hours Unrestricted from the outside | Tip Check out the "My Florist" sign near the northeast corner of 7th Avenue and McDowell Road. It marks the site of My Florist, the anchor store in a retail center that was built in 1947. There is no flower shop there today, but the sign continues to blossom (530 W McDowell Road, www.willophx.com/2023/05/10/my-florist-a-lasting-legacy).

16 Buddy Stubbs Bikes

The Southwest's largest collection of motorcycles

One of the few, if not only, motorcycle museums in the country that offers free admission, Buddy Stubbs Historical Motorcycle Museum is home to 135 motorcycles that are all still in working condition. The Buddy Stubbs Harley-Davidson dealership opened in 1966, with Motorcyclist Extraordinaire Buddy Stubbs still at the helm today – when he's not out riding on the open road. His sons Frank and Jack now also run operations.

Buddy grew up around motorcycles. His first experience was arriving at his parents' Harley-Davidson dealership as a 10-day-old baby in Decatur, Illinois. Baby Buddy would ride around town in a motorcycle sidecar with his mother until the family bought a car. Fast-forward to 1963, when Buddy, a privateer, not factory-sponsored, won the Daytona 100-Miler. In 1966, at 26 years old, he purchased a bankrupt Harley-Davidson dealership in Phoenix, and the rest is history.

The docents here are experienced motorcycle riders and friends of the family. They'll tell you all about the collection of street, racing, and military bikes. You'll also see a snowmobile, which is not something you see in Phoenix every day. The military bikes are on the second level, some of them from extremely limited series and therefore quite rare. On the first level, you'll find primarily street and racing bikes. Of course, Harley-Davidson bikes are prominent in the collection, but you'll also see Triumph, Indian, and other bikes from other parts of the world.

Also on view at the entrance to the museum is a recreation of the shattered bike that Evel Knievel (1938 – 2007) used for his world-famous 1967 Caesars Palace fountain jump in Las Vegas. Buddy owns every bike in this impressive collection of vintage motorcycles, which has grown to become the largest collection of street bikes and racing bikes in the Southwest. The onsite gift shop is also phenomenal and quite extensive.

Within the image, a placard reads:

1939
INDIAN
SPORT SCOUT
U.S.A.

S.V. 750 c.c.
V-TWIN

Address 13850 N Cave Creek Road, Phoenix, AZ 85022, +1 (602) 971-3400, www.buddystubbshd.com/museum, info@buddystubbs.com | **Getting there** By car, I-10 to north State Route-51, turn left onto E Cactus Road and right onto N Cave Creek Road | **Hours** Sat 11am–5pm | **Tip** Looking for a two-wheel experience but at a slower pace? Check out Scottsdale Segway Tours and wheel around charming Old Town Scottsdale. They also offer e-bike tours (4140 N Miller Road, Scottsdale, www.scottsdalesegwaytours.com).

17 __ Calvin C. Goode Building

Remarkable career begets building namesake

Calvin Coolidge Goode (1927–2020) was always soft-spoken, and many thought he was too timid to win an election for public office. Goode, who ran for Phoenix City Council on the slogan "Goode for Good Government," served for 11 consecutive terms, a record-breaking 22 years. He was the second Black American elected to the Council, and he made remarkable strides in his work, noted on the Calvin C. Goode Building's inscription: "Guided by a deeply held belief in God and in the equality of all people, his lifetime exemplified a powerful commitment to improving the quality of life in Phoenix, especially for young people."

In commemoration of Goode's many years of service to the city, the Phoenix Municipal Building was named in his honor. When the building was originally opened in 1963, architects Ed Varney and Ralph Haver delivered a design that is a pristine example of that era's thoughtful architecture, which won numerous prestigious awards. The structure's perimeter of 24-foot-tall arches, its tall, tilted windows, and vertical lines give it a monumental appearance. Surrounding the Goode Building are several other prominent landmarks, including the circular City of Phoenix Council Chambers, Phoenix City Hall, a time capsule scheduled to be opened in 2070, and a 1924 equestrian sculpture by the renowned Constance Whitney Warren titled *Lariat Cowboy.*

The annual Phoenix Human Rights Awards' Lifetime Achievement Award is bestowed on an individual who has "made Phoenix a better place to live through a lifelong dedication to promoting social and economic justice, defending civil rights, and enhancing the dignity of all people…nominations must emulate the lifelong dedication of Calvin C. Goode." Perhaps one of Goode's greatest accolades was that of being referred to by friends, coworkers, and the press as the "conscience of the Council."

Address 251 W Washington Street, Phoenix, AZ 85003, www.historicalleague.org/historymakers/calvin-c-goode | Getting there Valley Metro Light Rail to Jefferson/1st Avenue or Washington/Central Avenue; bus DASH to Washington Street & 4th Avenue | Hours Unrestricted from the outside | Tip On the east side of the Goode Building, you'll find César Chávez Memorial Plaza. Chávez (1927–1993) was a leader for civil rights, the Latino community, farm workers, and laborers, known for his nonviolent and successful efforts for social change. The plaza is host to Phoenix Earth Day and Cinco de Mayo celebrations (200 W Jefferson Street).

18__Cancer Survivors Park

Hopefully one day a historic relic

"There is no such thing as false hope for a cancer patient," said Richard A. Bloch, two-time cancer survivor, co-founder with his wife of the Cancer Hotline and co-founder with his brother of H&R Block, the international tax preparation company.

The Richard and Annette Bloch Cancer Survivors Park is something special. It's a beacon of hope, and, more importantly, it's one of encouragement. Noted on www.blochcancer.org, "Cancer Survivor Parks promote survivorship and provide common sense information that will guide and support the patient through his or her cancer journey." This park is one of twenty-four Richard and Annette Bloch Cancer Survivors Parks in the United States and Canada, and one of two in Arizona.

According to the same website, in 2024, nearly 20 million Americans with a history of serious cancer are alive today because they didn't give up hope and fought their disease. The parks have a common format, but each has design elements from its geographical locale. The highlight of the parks is a grouping of bronze sculptures by artist Victor Salmones (1937–1989), the most widely known sculptor living and working in Mexico during his lifetime. The collection is called *Cancer, There's Hope*. There are eight figures portraying the various stages of fighting cancer and the range of emotions on the path to survival. Of the 14 bronze plaques, 4 are inspirational, 10 are instructional, and all of them are comforting. One of the plaques cites "Knowledge" as a tool for survival.

This park is a block long, with numerous benches along its winding path, where visitors can relax and contemplate recovery and being cured. The beginning of the park is at McDowell Road, across from the Phoenix Art Museum, and it lets out at Burton Barr Central Library, which offers ample research opportunities for the "knowledge" needed in the fight against cancer.

Address 1428 N 1st Street, Phoenix, AZ 85004 | Getting there Valley Metro Light Rail to McDowell/Central Avenue; bus 0, 17 to Central Avenue & McDowell Road | Hours Unrestricted | Tip Nearby Italian restaurant, bar, and pizzeria Forno 301 is a true Italian dining experience, best enjoyed when it's busy (1616 N Central Avenue, #104, www.forno301.com).

19 Carnegie Public Library

Phoenix's first public library building

Known as the Father of Modern Philanthropy, industrialist Andrew Carnegie (1835–1919) funded the construction of nearly half the public libraries in the US between 1883 and 1929, including Phoenix's first public library building, funded in 1904. It was officially dedicated on February 14, 1908, exactly four years before Arizona was granted statehood. It's situated between the Arizona Capitol Museum (the former Capitol Building) and City Hall in downtown Phoenix.

The building, which still bears the original inscription CARNEGIE PUBLIC LIBRARY over its main entrance, served as the main branch of Phoenix public libraries until 1952, after 44 years of service. Since then, it has been the site for a state library, a senior center, a storage facility, an administration building, a homeless shelter, and a museum.

This stately library, made of red brick and 12-inch-thick walls, with a patina-green vaulted, domed roof, has changed little since its construction. The park around the library, however, was initially a horticultural experiment to determine which plant species would grow best in the desert climate. Once flanked by large walnut trees, the park still has some large, very old olive trees, which, surprisingly, grow very well in the desert, as well as a number of towering palm trees. Today, it's surrounded by brick pillars and a black fence but stands as majestic as ever, having undergone a significant renovation. The project was overseen by architect Gerald A. Doyle, who also worked on the Arizona State Capitol restoration project. In 1989, he would receive the Governor's Award for Historic Preservation.

Other significant contributors to Phoenix public libraries include Maie Bartlett Heard (1868–1951), cofounder of the Heard Museum, and Alfred Knight (1874–1958), who donated 3,000 rare books, including a set of Shakespeare's texts from the 1600s.

Address 1101 W Washington Street, Phoenix, AZ 85007 | Getting there Bus I-10, I-17, DASH, GAL to Washington Street & 12th Avenue | Hours Unrestricted from the outside | Tip Bring a book and have a seat at First Draft Book Bar, a wine, beer, coffee, and pastry bar inside the Phoenix location of the legendary Changing Hands Bookstore (300 W Camelback Road, www.changinghands.com/first-draft-book-bar).

20__ Centennial Time Capsule
To be opened…in 100 years

On the occasion of the 100th anniversary of Phoenix being selected as a townsite, the City of Phoenix buried and sealed a time capsule that was to be opened 100 years later. The selection date was on Friday, November 25, 1870, and so the time capsule ceremony was Wednesday, November 25, 1970, with an opening ceremony scheduled for Tuesday, November 25, 2070, as clearly stated on the mammoth plate covering the site.

The time capsule was placed at the northwest corner of City Hall and contains centennial copies of *The Arizona Republic* newspaper, *The Phoenix Gazette*, *PHOENIX* magazine, and *Arizona Highways* magazine, as well as a key to the city. Also in the capsule is a Native American rabbit stick, a curved, wooden stick weighted on one end and used to hunt small game, a nod to the indigenous peoples who lived where Phoenix now towers.

At the top of the long, rectangular plaque is a large copy of the commemorative medal, a collectible coin, to honor the Phoenix Centennial. It was sculpted by Phoenician Don Dow, whose initials you can see in the lower right corner of the medallion: "DDow ©". The front of the collectible coin (and top of the capsule) reads, "Phoenix, Arizona – 1870 – Centennial 1970."

There were 2,000-plus people, including 50 surviving pioneers of the Arizona Territory, at the Centennial Dinner the evening before the time capsule ceremony that late morning. The time capsule also contains messages to the future in the form of letters from Arizona Governor Jack Williams and Phoenix Mayor John Driggs. Driggs' letter, addressed to the future mayor of Phoenix in 2070, said: "I hope you will have built upon our future as we built upon our past." During the Centennial Dinner, then-Governor Barry Goldwater predicted that Phoenix might become the fifth or sixth largest city in the country. Today it is, in fact, the fifth largest.

Address 200 W Jefferson Street, Phoenix, AZ 85003 | Getting there Valley Metro Light Rail to Jefferson/1st Avenue | Hours Unrestricted | Tip If you're fascinated by time travel and enjoy a delicious taco, check out the former Bethel Methodist Church building, today the fabulous Taco Guild. On display are the contents of the church's time capsules, dating to 1893 and 1955 (546 E Osborn Road, www.tacoguild.com).

CENTENNIAL TIME CAPSULE

COMMEMORATING THE 100TH ANNIVERSARY

OF THE

SELECTION OF THE PHOENIX TOWNSITE

DEPOSITED NOVEMBER 25, 1970

TO BE OPENED NOVEMBER 25, 2070

21 Centennial Way

100 years of Arizona history in plain sight

Hiding in plain sight is a fascinating project that would become Centennial Way, though if you visited the Arizona Capitol regularly just prior to 2012, the centennial of Arizona's being granted statehood, you would definitely have noticed it. Centennial Way was created for Arizona's 100th birthday and to celebrate the state, culminating in a celebration event on February 14, 2012.

Centennial Way is a multi-faceted, cultural adventure that stretches along Washington Street between W 7th and W 19th Avenues, the historic corridor that connects downtown Phoenix to the State Capitol. Washington Street is the North/South delineator for the city, as Washington and Central is the geographical center of the city. The street intersections of Centennial Way feature the state flag with its bright colors, and also the dates of statehood and the 1912 – 2012 centennial.

Along the way, you will see wayfinding signage with the always helpful "You Are Here" notations. This avenue is divided into sections. The section nearest the Capitol recognizes the 22 Native American tribes across the State of Arizona in sculptural pylons with curved steel spires and laser-cut banners around concrete bases with each tribe's name and seal. The Arizona Displays and County Displays are intermingled heading toward W 7th Avenue. There are 15 counties in Arizona (compared to Texas' 250-plus counties), eight of which are named for Native American tribes. The tallest installations are the Arizona Displays, which feature various aspects of the state's history, distant and contemporary.

One of the things that you will learn along Centennial Way are the various nicknames for Arizona. One of them is the Valentine State, because its statehood anniversary fell on Valentine's Day. Arizona has also been called the Grand Canyon State since the 1930s – that nickname was officially signed into law in 2011.

Address Washington Street between W 7th & W 19th Avenues, Phoenix, AZ 85034 | Getting there Valley Metro Light Rail to 12th Avenue/Washington; bus 1 to 7th Avenue & Washington Street | Hours Unrestricted | Tip Venture to Zuzu, a mid-century modern restaurant in the historic Hotel Valley Ho (6850 E Main Street, Scottsdale, www.hotelvalleyho.com/zuzu).

22 — The Circle of Life

Dark history of forced assimilation

The beauty of Steele Indian School Park belies the dark history it commemorates. The Federal Government purchased 160 acres of farmland in 1890, and opened the Phoenix Indian School in 1891. At its peak, there were 900 Native American children attending the school. Government agents forcibly took many of the students from their families in 23 different states to attend the school. They were required to cut ties with their own cultures and assimilate to the militaristic form of education here. There were over 523 such schools across the United States.

The horrendous abuse and suffering that these government-funded schools inflicted on Native American children is well documented today. However, some students achieved remarkable things. Some learned instruments they'd never seen as part of the assimilation process, and the award-winning marching band served as President Wilson's honor guard at the Paris Peace Conference following the Great War. A placard on the fountain at Memorial Hall (1922) lists the names of students who enlisted in the Army and Navy, including Lee Rainbow and Wallace Antone, both killed in action during World War I.

The Circle of Life is a circular walkway, 600 feet in diameter, with etched, large-scale dates from the founding of the Indian School in 1891 through its eventual closing in 1990. Twenty-four interpretive pylons discuss the life of the students and their many accomplishments.

When the Government closed the school after a century, the land was obtained by the City of Phoenix. In 2001 Steele Indian School Park opened on the site. It is dedicated to making the 75 acres of land and its historic buildings an educational and recreational experience. The park is named for Phoenix-born Horace C. Steele, the successful businessperson and philanthropist, whose foundation contributed $2.5 million towards the creation of the park.

Address 300 E Indian School Road, Phoenix, AZ 85012, +1 (602) 534-4810, www.phoenix.gov/parks/parks/alphabetical/s-parks/steele-indian-school | **Getting there** Bus 41 to Indian School Road & 3rd Street | **Hours** Daily 6am–10pm | **Tip** Learn more about life at Phoenix Indian School in the exhibit "Away From Home" at the Heard Museum (2301 N Central Avenue, www.heard.org).

23   Copper Company Locomotive

A relic from the early days of mining

Arizona produces more copper and non-fuel minerals than any other state in the country. The Arizona Copper Company's Locomotive #2 was part of the early days of copper mining in the state. It is now proudly displayed in front of the Polly Rosenbaum Building, formerly the El Zariba Shrine Auditorium for the Phoenix chapter of Shriners International.

That Shrine chapter was chartered in 1896, and their auditorium was built in 1921. It was designed by architects Lescher & Mahoney, who designed the Morenci Copper Mine staff housing (1967) in Morenci, Arizona, where Locomotive #2 had been in use. You'll notice how tiny this locomotive is at only 17 feet long and 5.5 feet wide. It weighs 11 tons, compared with modern locomotives that can weigh up to 400 tons, according to the Engine Technology Forum. Locomotive #2 was abandoned in 1923, but luckily, you can admire it here today.

Polly Rosenbaum (1899–2003), the building's namesake, had worked for a copper company in her early years and would later become Arizona's longest-serving state legislator. She was inducted into the Arizona Women's Hall of Fame in 2006. The 18,000-square-foot building used to be the home of the Arizona Mining and Mineral Museum, which is why some of the other artifacts and murals found here are mining related. Look for the excavator bucket that could hold a dozen people, and the tire from a Kubota mining truck that's bigger than an SUV.

This historic building is the future home of The Arizona Mining, Mineral and Natural Resources Education (AMMNRE) Museum, through the University of Arizona. Its objectives will be to promote the state's natural resource heritage and future through education, research, and outreach.

Address 1502 W Washington Street, Phoenix, AZ 85007, www.ammnre.arizona.edu/collection, cscarter@arizona.edu | Getting there Bus 15, 514, 521, 522, 531, 533. 535, DASH bus to Washington Street & 15th Avenue | Hours Unrestricted from the outside | Tip Visit the Arizona Railway Museum, where you can explore a vast collection of railway cars, including a dozen passenger cars that you can walk through (330 E Ryan Road, Chandler, www.azrymuseum.org).

24 Cosanti

A living testament to Paolo Soleri's "arcology"

Perhaps you have heard of the world-famous bells crafted by Cosanti Originals? Today, you can explore the working, thriving community and the place where Cosanti bells are made in a space designed by architect and urban planner Paolo Soleri (1919–2013).

Soleri arrived in the US in 1947 from Italy to apprentice under Frank Lloyd Wright, but they had very different ideas about the future of American cities. Soleri's vision was for "urban implosion," a compact and vertically dense environment that emphasized people's connection to one another and to nature, and what would become known as "arcology," the meeting of architecture and ecology. The structures you see here today were built mostly in the 1950s and early 60s using an "earth-casting" technique. They've held up to the test of time quite remarkably.

Visitors to Cosanti are welcome to venture through portions of the Cosanti campus while shopping for their very own, one-of-a-kind Cosanti Originals bell. Among those areas are the Bell Gallery, with a roof shaped like a fish – you will easily see it when standing inside – and the North Apse, the only apse facing north, to take advantage of year-round shade.

Other areas are accessible on a guided tour, which usually includes a live bronze-pouring demonstration. Up to three times per day Monday through Friday, you can learn and see how 100 pounds of bronze is heated and poured. Visitors are guided through Soleri's first ceramics studio in the South Apse; the Cat Cast, named not for feline friends but the Caterpillar tractor required to assist with construction; the Solari home they built for themselves but never lived in; the swimming pool; the barrel vault; the Pumpkin Apse, where Solari would lecture; and several other places on this highly informative, hour-long tour. Some of these spaces have only recently opened to the public for the first time in decades.

Address 6433 E Doubletree Ranch Road, Paradise Valley, AZ 85253, +1 (480) 948-6145, www.cosanti.com, tours@cosanti.com | Getting there By car, take I-10 east to State Route 51 North. Take Exit 5 then right on E Lincoln Drive. Left on N Tatum Boulevard, then right on E Doubletree Ranch Road | Hours Mon–Sat 9am–5pm, Sun 11am–5pm, see website for tour schedule | Tip Built around the same time, the Bowlero building on Bethany Home Road is a "striking" example of mid-century modern architecture (1919 W Bethany Home Road, www.bowlero.com/location/bowlero-christown).

25__Curious Nature

Tarot, taxidermy, and tea leaves

A Goth kid who would learn veterinary medical science and who also appreciates a Victorian aesthetic, Mason Conway took a risk in February 2014. He invested his savings to launch Curious Nature, a shop filled with items that spoke to his unique set of interests and billed as "A Fine Natural History Emporium." If you've ever wondered about the Victorian-era aristocrats' and commoners' deep interest in death, curiosities, and the natural world, look to Curious Nature. You'll find collections of seashells, exotic plants, and some magnificent specimens documenting natural history, as well as a few from the fantastical realm.

Whether you are creating a space for quiet contemplation or study or for socializing, this shopping destination can help you appoint your space with an array of conversation starters. One such item here is a shell of the cone snail, one of the most venomous animal on the planet. That creature doesn't live in Arizona, but one of the fabulously attractive aspects of Curious Nature is that a vast majority of its offerings come from the far corners of the globe, as well as some closer locales, too.

If you like to write, you'll discover a plethora of naughty, not-so-subtle greeting cards – they're hilarious if you're light-hearted – and other clever gift items. Enjoy meandering up and down the rows of items ranging from tarot, magic, the occult, and astrological themes, to candles, octopus finger puppets, sea-life watercolors, blown-glass mushrooms, and unicorns.

The shop offers a breadth of classes and special events too. Classes might include reading tea leaves and astrology, and events have included speaking engagements with a local coroner and other such themes. There are also taxidermy classes, during which you have the highly unique opportunity to recreate the mythical jackalope, a creature first "discovered" in 1932. You get to take yours home.

Address 4346 N 7th Avenue, Phoenix, AZ 85013, +1 (602) 314-4346, curiousnatureshop.com, phoenix@curiousnatureshop.com | Getting there Bus 8 to N 7th & Glenrosa Avenues | Hours Mon–Fri 11am–6pm, Sat & Sun 11am–5pm | Tip At the Arizona Museum of Natural History, the dinosaurs are literally bursting through the side of the building. You can commune with the T-Rex, Apatosaurus (previously known as Brontosaurus), and Triceratops, as well as many other lesser-known dinos (53 N Macdonald, Mesa, www.arizonamuseumofnaturalhistory.org).

26 Cutler-Plotkin Jewish Heritage Center

The first synagogue in Phoenix

The Cutler-Plotkin Jewish Heritage Center is a place where people from all walks of life can go to learn about the Jewish experience in Arizona.

Today's heritage center buildings were constructed in 1922 for the first synagogue in Phoenix, serving the Congregation Beth Israel, later known as Temple Beth Israel. In 1957, the site became the first Chinese language Baptist church. Look for a cornerstone with "The Chinese Baptist Church" engraved in English and Chinese characters. In 1981, it became Iglesia Bautista Central, or Central Baptist Church, serving a Hispanic congregation. Then, in 2001, it was purchased and fully renovated by the Arizona Jewish Historical Society. The first holiday celebrated in the renewed space was Sukkot.

The new facility was named for Bettie and James Cutler, parents of benefactor Larry Cutler, and Rabbi Albert Plotkin, who came to Phoenix in 1955. For more than four generations, he officiated over consecrations; bat, bar, and b'nai mitzvahs, including Larry's bar mitzvah in 1965; weddings; and funerals.

The Center has a wide range of offerings, including exhibitions, cultural activities, and tours (by reservation). There is a monthly book discussion group and a monthly documentary film series, free to the public, as well as live music events. This multi-cultured, historic place of worship has been placed on the Phoenix Historic Property Register and the National Register of Historic Places.

The Hilton Family Holocaust Education Center, in a large new building behind Phoenix's first synagogue, is deep into the planning stage. With the Center's central downtown location, easy access via Valley Metro's light rail service and ample parking, the center is poised to enhance the educational experience of students and the public.

Address 122 E Culver Street, Phoenix, AZ 85004, +1 (602) 241-7870, www.azjhs.org, tours@azjhs.org | Getting there Valley Metro Light Rail to McDowell/Central Avenue; bus 0 to Central Avenue & Culver Street | Hours By appointment only; see website for event schedule | Tip For mouthwatering deli sandwiches in the valley, head to Miracle Mile Deli, where you can order a Reuben, hot pastrami, brisket, and so much more (4433 N 16th Street, www.miraclemiledeli.com).

27 __ Del Monte Market
The oldest market in Arizona

On a street corner, with a backdrop of the majestic mountains that make up the southern Phoenix horizon, stands Del Monte Market, a brick convenience store that has been in business since its establishment in 1908. The business' 120th anniversary is fast approaching, and it was around four years before Arizona was even a state. It's the oldest market in the state, according to local articles and Will, the market's owner.

Designed in the handsome Mission Revival style, the exterior appears to have been refreshed and well kept, including its decorative brickwork. The sign over the front door reaches toward the street corner in a diagonal fashion and is more reminiscent of a rusted sign you might see on Historic Route 66. Of course, having been around since the early 1900s, this building is indeed historic.

Dating to the days when Del Monte Market was called Brutcher's Store and sold groceries, fresh meats, and vegetables, this popular neighborhood destination continues to serve the people in the neighboring areas. Today, its exterior advertises beer, wine, and groceries in paint on the side of the building. But you will find more at this market than you might expect. The shelves hold the typical convenience store staples, including soda, coffee, and ice cream, of course, but you will also find souvenirs – there's an excellent ball cap selection – as well as local snacks, regional libation mixers, lottery tickets, and even motor oil.

This was a meeting place from its beginnings way back in the day – you can still see cowboys on horseback gathering in front of the shop – and there's the occasional classic car show. For a modest space, there's a lot going on here. Visit with realistic expectations though, as it's not a state-of-the-art shopping destination. It's a corner market that's been around for a very long time, with customers who have been devoted for decades.

Address 2659 W Dobbins Road, Phoenix, AZ 85041 | **Getting there** By car, take W Dobbins Road west to S 27th Avenue | **Hours** Daily 8am – 9pm | **Tip** With its own historic ties, building, and family owners, El Portal Mexican Restaurant is welcoming and delicious. Be sure to admire the magnificent murals inside (117 W Grant Street, www.elportalmexicanrestaurant.org).

28_Disco Dragon

The décor brings you in, the food brings you back

Forget the mirror balls, as festive as they are, and enjoy a spinning, mirrored mannequin instead. Actually, it's one mannequin, but split in half and hanging on opposite ends of the dining space known as Disco Dragon, the perfect start to a night on the town or the perfect place for late night eats. And don't fret about the disco balls – you'll find them here too. They are in their native habitat (hanging from the ceiling) but they're planters. This modestly sized dining destination has bar seating, where you will want to order food, as your eyes wander through the mural of Greek gods behind the bar. There are also comfy booths, so bring your friends.

Now that you have a lay of the land, it helps to know where you're going when heading here. The signage isn't as subtle as it once was, but still, if you blink, you just might miss it. Look for the bright green neon "OPEN" sign in the window.

Inside, you'll find a bar that's flooded with the same neon green, as well as bright purple. This "modern izakaya" in downtown Phoenix, along Roosevelt Row, features Filipino and Chinese flavors with influences by chefs Kevin Rosales – who used to run a crazy-popular food truck – and Bob Tam. Everything is delicious on the Pan-Asian menu, which is designed to complement the craft cocktails (some with large, branded ice cubes), sake, and Asian beers. Definitely try the hand-rolled pork lumpia to share, but you'll wish they were all yours. They're Filipino-inspired and come with a sweet chili sauce.

Whether you have to go or not, you won't want to miss the bathrooms. Look up at the ceiling, where you will discover even more bright green neon, and yourself, to infinity! The ceilings are mirrored. Disco Dragon is great for a date night, hanging out with friends, or happy hour with your coworkers who like good eats. Disco Dragon does not take reservations but you're always welcome.

Address 509 E Roosevelt Street, Phoenix, AZ 85004, www.thosepourbastards.com/disco-dragon, info@discodragonphx.com | **Getting there** Bus 7 to Roosevelt & 7th Streets | **Hours** Daily 6pm – 1am | **Tip** Check out Arizona Wilderness Brewing just down the street. Their beer saves water through the malt they source (201 E Roosevelt Street, www.azwbeer.com).

29 Dobbins Lookout
Petroglyphs, saguaros, and scenic views

At 2,330 feet, Dobbins Lookout is the highest point on South Mountain that locals and tourists can visit, and it's worth the drive. Once you're there, either via Summit Road or one of the numerous hiking trails, you have opened yourself to a world of wonders. South Mountain Park and Preserve celebrated its 100th birthday in 2024. It spans across three mountain ranges: Ma Ha Tauk, Gila, and Guadalupe. The most recognizable feature of South Mountain is the iconic communications antennae atop Mount Suappoa.

What's not well known is the cornucopia of features this park offers and some of its fascinating history. The original 13,000 acres were purchased in 1924 from the Federal Government at the approximate price of $1.25 per acre (the national average for farmland then was $54 per acre).

That same year, President Calvin Coolidge signed into law the Indian Citizenship Act, which granted US citizenship to all Native Americans. South Mountain Park today is an impressive 16,000 acres and can boast that it is one of the largest municipally managed parks in the country. There are more than 100 miles of hiking trails and access points from nearly every direction.

From Dobbins Lookout, visitors get to enjoy unobstructed, panoramic views of Phoenix, and beyond. Look for the sizable stone platform. On a cylindrical pillar is a large directional marker that points out what you are seeing, from downtown Phoenix to the Superstition Mountains. A gift from Nathan Straus, Jr. (1889–1961), it was dedicated in February 1960. While you're hiking, look for the thousands of petroglyphs created by the Native Americans who once thrived on this land. There are structures in the park that date to the 1930s, when 4,000 men worked here with the Civilian Conservation Corps, a post-Great Depression work program. And this is a fantastic place to take a selfie with a saguaro cactus.

Address 10919 S Central Avenue, Phoenix, AZ 85042, +1 (602) 262-7393,
www.phoenix.gov/parks/trails/locations/south-mountain | Getting there By car, drive south
on S Central Avenue to destination | Hours See website for seasonal hours | Tip Now that
you've seen the city from South Mountain, head up to North Mountain Park National
Trail and see the Valley of the Sun from a totally different perspective (10600 N 7th Street,
www.alltrails.com/trail/us/arizona/north-mountain-national-trail--4).

30___Dolly Steamboat

Cruise on Canyon Lake

Before the advent of trains, cars, and airplanes, rivers were used as one of the primary means of transportation, including luxury travel. Today, as in yesteryear, steamboats are a fun mode of exploring locales that you may not have seen before or may not be able to readily visit otherwise. In this case, you don't have to go all the way to the Mississippi River to catch a ride on one. For a scenic nature cruise, a delightful twilight dinner cruise, or a romantic astronomy cruise, come aboard the Dolly Steamboat.

Founded in 1987 by Roger and Margie Grimh, who moved to the area from Wisconsin, Dolly Steamboat today is managed by their children. Captain Jeff Grimh also serves as narrator during the cruises, gifting passengers a front row seat to the picturesque aftermath of active volcanoes 25 million years ago. Cindi DeLoseur is the delightful "voice" behind the marketing and email confirmations, and also co-CEO and co-owner.

"You cannot surprise an individual more than twice with the same marvel," wrote Mark Twain in *Life on the Mississippi* (1883). While Twain was inarguably brilliant, the beauty and majesty of Canyon Lake questions this thought. Even the drive here on State Route 88 with the Superstition Mountains on the horizon is mesmerizing.

Canyon Lake is tucked away in Tonto National Forest, the largest national forest in Arizona at more than 2.9 million acres. These canyons are home to desert bighorn sheep, bald eagles, osprey, mallards, and so much more. On the flora spectra, cruise-goers will enjoy saguaro cactus, ocotillo, teddy bear cholla, prickly pear cactus, and palo verde, the Arizona State Tree, to name only a few found along the 28.3 miles of towering, neck-bending shoreline. Particularly spectacular on the dinner cruise, says Captain Jeff, are the Four Peaks Mountains at sunset. You can enjoy a libation or two while you cruise across a lake that feels like a river.

Address 16802 AZ-88, Apache Junction, AZ 85117, +1 (480) 827-9144,
www.dollysteamboat.com, customerservice@dollysteamboat.net | Getting there By car,
take I-10 east to US-60, then take exit 196 to AZ-88 (E Apache Trail) to destination |
Hours See website for cruise schedule | Tip Nearby is Goldfield Ghost Town, where you
can drink in a saloon, pan for gold, shop in a general store, and see an Old West gunfight
(4650 N Mammoth Mine Road, Apache Junction, goldfieldghosttown.com).

31 Dulceria La Bonita

Celebrations are better with a giant piñata

The joy on the kids' faces when they see a giant piñata at their party is unmatched and wonderful to see. The excitement on grownups' faces when they see a giant piñata at their party is a sign that stories are about to be made.

A tradition in some cultures, a novelty in others, a celebration with a piñata is always a great time. And if you have never been to Dulceria La Bonita, you're in for a real treat. They're more than a party supplies store. They're more than a candy and party snacks supplies store. They're more than a piñata store. They're all of the above and more. This is the ultimate treasure trove of traditional and imported Mexican candy and culture.

When you first walk into this wholesale shop, you may not immediately realize what you are about to experience. It will gradually unfold, aisle after aisle after aisle. The adobe brown building with bright pink signage feels much larger on the inside than it looks like from the outside. If you are looking for party supplies, turn left. If you are looking for candy and ice cream supplies, turn right.

The GIANT piñatas are on the party supplies side, but they may as well have their own wing of the building. They come in all shapes and sizes, but mostly large, extra-large, and gigantic. There are classic stars and burros, as well as unicorns and other characters. Bursting with color, the piñatas are all around on top of the shelves and hanging overhead.

And what's the perfect party treat in the middle of the Sonoran Desert? Ice cream. There are lots of ice cream flavors here, including a full line of Frutifresca ice cream: lemon lime, coconut and cream, and many more. When you come here to select the perfect giant piñata for your special occasion, be sure to drive the big car or borrow your neighbor's SUV. You will definitely leave with more than you were planning to buy. And that's a good thing here.

Address 2311 N 35th Avenue, Phoenix, AZ 85009, +1 (602) 626-8334, www.labonita.store |
Getting there Bus 35 to 35th Avenue & Encanto Boulevard | Hours Daily 6am–8:30pm |
Tip Originally designed and built by Disney (no current affiliation), Makutu's Island is host
to "magical" creatures on a playground that features a four-story slide (6919 W Ray Road,
Chandler, www.makutusisland.com).

32 Elvis Chapel

This movie set survived two fires

You don't have to go all the way to Las Vegas to get married by Elvis – more precisely, an Elvis impersonator. You can exchange your nuptials right here in front of the King of Rock-n-Roll at the Elvis Memorial Chapel at the Superstition Mountain Museum.

Actually, it's a statue of Elvis, singing, ironically. This chapel was part of the movie set for *Charro*, the only film Elvis made when he did not sing. This non-singing Elvis film was one of the 31 feature films the King of Rock & Roll made. In the statue, Elvis is playing a blue guitar, but he's unfortunately not wearing blue suede shoes. That's okay, as his stance is the iconic "Elvis the Pelvis," a moniker used by millions of his fans. *Charro* was also the only film in which Elvis sported a beard.

The chapel's setting is picturesque. Nearby is the Apacheland barn and a horse-drawn stagecoach. In the background are the majestic Superstition Mountains. After you've taken your photos of the setting, you'll pass through a white picket fence. The front doors are flanked by saguaro cactus, and the inside is lined with church pews. The walls of the chapel feature Elvis movie posters. You may see some familiar titles.

Harkening back to the golden years of the Westerns, Apacheland is where this chapel was originally located. Apacheland was the movie set for any "Wild West" town, and Western movies were filmed here for 45 years. This chapel and one other structure, a barn, survived two fires, the last one taking the rest of the movie set town with it. If you're a true fan of the Western, be sure to make a point to see Frederic Remington's *Stampede* bronze sculpture (reproduction) while you're here. This classic is beautifully situated with the Superstition Mountains in the background. You also have the fantastic opportunity to learn about the Lost Dutchman and some of the mystery and speculation of 'lost' gold.

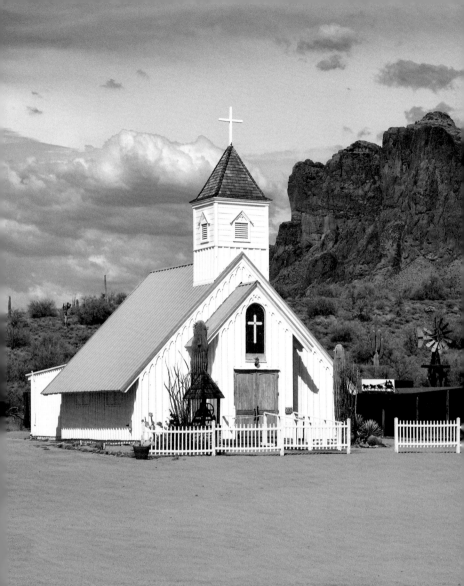

Address 4087 E Apache Trail, Apache Junction, AZ 85119, +1 (480) 983-4888, superstitionmountainlostdutchmanmuseum.org | Getting there By car, take I-10 east to US-60, then take exit 196 to AZ-88 (E Apache Trail) to destination | Hours Daily 9am–3pm | Tip Opened in 1965 and still in operation today, the Arizona Veterans Memorial Coliseum on the grounds of today's Arizona State Fair is where Elvis performed when he kicked off his first tour of the 1970s and returned to Phoenix in 1973. Both were, of course, sold-out concerts (1826 W McDowell Road, www.azstatefair.com).

33 — Encanto Carousel

Locals saved this historic treasure

In a 2015 *Phoenix Magazine* article, attorney Peter Spaw said, "No matter how cool you were, you learned from the carousel that there was a place in life for art, music, and simple beauty." Spaw had ridden on the Encanto Carousel when he was a kid, as have his kids and grandkids. Made by the Allan Herschell Company, the oldest continuously operating carousel in Arizona was nearly lost. But its history was redirected thanks to the determined efforts of locals.

The Kiddieland amusement park opened in 1948, with a brand-new carousel boasting 20 shiny, hand-carved horses, along with other "pint-sized" rides. In 1984, plans were made to refurbish the northern side of Encanto Park, including Kiddieland. But Kiddieland's owners stated that their business could not withstand the 16-month closure during the renovation. The rides were sold at auction in November 1986 in less than an hour.

Even before the auction, the story pulled at locals' heartstrings, and a group of mothers created the Encanto Carousel Fund. The carousel's new owner offered to sell it to them for $55,000, the same price paid at auction, if they raised the money by December 31. With only days to go, they collected the full amount needed to purchase the beloved carousel, and then they also raised the funds for its restoration. Local artist Maggie Keane rebuilt damaged wood and repainted the horses and the rounding boards. The carousel glowed at the opening of the new Enchanted Island Amusement Park in 1991.

Phoenix celebrated the carousel's 50th birthday in 1998, when it became a permanent fixture in Encanto Park. Throughout the decades, the Encanto Carousel has been the centerpiece for thousands of birthdays, reunions, and first dates, as well as the backdrop for quite a few weddings. Whatever the celebration, the endearing and enduring carousel brings out the kid in all of us.

Address 1202 W Encanto Boulevard, Phoenix, AZ 85007, +1 (602) 254-1200, www.enchantedisland.com, info@enchantedisland.com | **Getting there** By car, drive north on N 7th Avenue, then turn left on W Encanto Boulevard | **Hours** See website for seasonal hours | **Tip** Carousel Arcade Bar is fun for all ages, just at different times. In the afternoon all ages are welcome, and in the evening it's 21-plus only. Let the good times roll! (6770 N Sunrise Boulevard, Glendale, www.carouselarcadebar.com)

34 Estrella Star Tower

A tribute to stargazing cultures

"Astronomy is the oldest of all sciences, yet never has it been more exciting than it is today," said Eric Chaisson in *Astronomy Today*.

Come find yourself at *Estrella Star Tower*. It's a place of contemplation of your place in the Milky Way galaxy. And it's a place of honor to the ancient Native American civilizations who made the same introspective and stellar explorations on these very grounds. As you approach the Star Tower from any direction, you experience a dramatic sense of arrival, whether the tower is set upon a vivid blue Arizona sky or a still, starry evening.

This 50-foot spiral tower was placed in the Sonoran Desert Valley, the West Valley to be more specific, as a marker that you have arrived at the master-planned community of Estrella in Goodyear, Arizona. It was made by the development company Newland Communities. Intended to be an "attraction" of sorts for the Estrella community, it has become a destination for romantic date nights, a memorable place for wedding proposals, and a revered space for introspection. And it also offers spectacular views of the Estrella Mountains, as well as the beautiful nighttime desert sky.

Although you might convince an unknowing person that the tower is ancient, especially given its astronomical purpose, it's not very old at all, relatively speaking. Even the teenagers coming here on dates were not even born yet when Estrella Star Tower was dedicated in late spring 2007.

On the floor at the top of the tower is an etched, abstract depiction of our spiral Milky Way galaxy. Its shape is surprisingly accurate, featuring a bar center and two major arms. The spiral tower is made of stacked stone and massive slabs of rusted steel, with a vertical steel sail on top pointing to the stars. The Tower has LED lights throughout that create their own constellations after the sun has retired for the evening. Come stargaze.

Address 8614 Estrella Parkway, Goodyear, AZ 85338 | **Getting there** By car, take
I-10 to exit 128 and go south on N Litchfield Road, turn right onto W NC 85, and left
onto Estrella Parkway | **Hours** Daily 10am–5pm, unrestricted from the outside | **Tip**
Nearby Estrella Mountain Regional Park is the second largest park in Metro Phoenix
and a great place to see spring wildflowers. You'll find more than 33 miles of trails for
hiking, mountain biking, and horseback riding (14805 W Vineyard Avenue, Goodyear,
www.maricopacountyparks.net/park-locator/estrella-mountain-regional-park).

35 First Christian Church

A born-again Frank Lloyd Wright

As you travel north on 7th Avenue, through downtown, past midtown, well into suburbia, and past countless palm trees and hundreds of manicured xeriscape yards, and out of the blue Arizona sky, you'll spot the two spectacular, towering spires of First Christian Church, founded in 1952. They are unmistakably inspired by world-famous architect and former Phoenix resident Frank Lloyd Wright (1867–1959).

In fact, the original design for this stunning place of worship was indeed created by Wright. In 1949, Southwest Christian Seminary in Phoenix commissioned him to design a Classical University with multiple structures on an 80-acre complex. The seminary ceased operations before its building could be built, and the design was made public in 1950.

In 1971, the design, which had been almost lost to obscurity, was resurrected. Governor Jack Williams (1909–1998) and Wright's Scottsdale-born wife Olgivanna Lloyd Wright (1998–1985) were among the dignitaries who spoke at the sanctuary's dedication in February 1973. When First Christian Church had first decided they wanted to use Wright's design, they had to get permission from the Frank Lloyd Wright Foundation and Mrs. Wright. She insisted that they follow the design specifications to the letter, which made for a magnificent, true, Wright-designed work of art and architecture to admire in north Central Phoenix.

The structures have Wright trademarks in his concrete-and-stone aesthetic. This design includes 20 tons of rock mined from the Arizona desert. The sanctuary features stained glass imported from France, Belgium, and Italy that was assembled in Tempe. The 120-foot-tall, freestanding bell tower, which is what immediately catches your attention, has an alloy skeleton that supports the structure's 304 tons of concrete, stone, and steel. The delight here is finding a genuine Wright design hidden in plain sight.

Address 6750 N 7th Avenue, Phoenix, AZ 85013, +1 (602) 246-9206, www.fccphx.com, info@fccphx.com | Getting there Bus 8 to 7th Avenue & Ocotillo Road | Hours Unrestricted from the outside, tours by reservation | Tip Continue going north to Sonoran Preserve to explore the open desert. This locale offers 36 miles of trails on 9,600 acres, with three trailheads (Desert Vista Trailhead, 1600 E Sonoran Desert Drive, www.phoenix.gov/parks/trails/locations/sonoran-preserve).

36 Flite Goodyear

Offices, radar, aircraft, blimp, tires, cotton

What do cotton and supersonic strategic reconnaissance aircraft have in common? They both have roots in Goodyear, Arizona. Paul Weeks Litchfield, native of New York, graduate of MIT, and CEO of Goodyear Tire & Rubber, garnered a patent in 1903 for the first tubeless automobile tire. In 1916, he purchased land near Phoenix that would later become Goodyear, AZ. And he established long-staple cotton farms, a crop used to reinforce the rubber in Goodyear tires.

Situated between Phoenix-Goodyear Airport and Litchfield Road, Flite Goodyear is an office, retail, and industrial complex. One of the first things you'll notice here is the 40-foot-wide,16-foot-tall pictorial of an original painting by Phoenix artist Randall Hedden. Facing Litchfield Road in the shadow of the water tower over Goodyear's technology corridor, the mural depicts the mysterious and mesmerizing SR-71 Blackbird, one of the most recognizable aircraft ever built.

This rendering of the high-altitude, supersonic spy plane is the first in an art series that portrays the fascinating history of this particular site. It's also a nod to the site's radar-research background. Synthetic Aperture Radar (SAR) used on the SR-71 was invented by engineer Carl Wiley at Goodyear Aircraft in the early 1950s.

During World War II, Goodyear Aircraft Company, a separate operating division of Goodyear Tire & Rubber Co., built Corsair airplanes for more than 20 different aircraft models. This is also the site where Goodyear-Zeppelin Corporation, founded by Litchfield, built Goodyear blimps for the US Navy. In preparation to create the mural for Flite Goodyear, Hedden, who researches all his art subjects, visited the Pima Air & Space Museum in Tucson, Arizona to see an SR-71 Blackbird up close. His imagination took him first to the upper atmosphere before returning to Phoenix to create his eye-catching, welcoming image.

Address 1300 S Litchfield Road, Goodyear, AZ 85338, https://flitegoodyear.colliers.com | Getting there By car, take I-10 to N Litchfield Road and turn south to destination | Hours Unrestricted from the outside | Tip The neighboring Phoenix-Goodyear Airport was once known as Litchfield Naval Air Facility and served as home to the US Navy Blue Angels from 1962 to 1966 (1658 S Litchfield Road, Goodyear, www.goodyearairport.com).

37 Flying V Cabin
The bloodiest family feud in history

The Pleasant Valley War was the bloodiest family feud in American history. With more casualties than the infamous Hatfield-McCoys and more violent than the gunfight at the O.K. Corral, the Tewksbury-Graham range war is the deadliest such conflict in US history, with 35 to 50 estimated deaths. The Flying V Cabin, former home of John Tewksbury and site of some of the killings, was relocated from Pleasant Valley, today's Young, Arizona in Gila County, to the Pioneer Living History Museum, which focuses on Arizona's pioneer and territorial years, 1863 to 1912.

The Flying V Cabin is one of several surviving original structures from Arizona's pioneer days. One of the notable features of this cabin is its horizontal slits for rifles and guns, a protective measure should the cabin be surrounded, which did happen. After John Tewksbury's death, George Newton and J. J. Vosberg bought this cabin and used it as a ranch building and later as a cabin for a line rider, a ranch hand who patrols property boundaries.

This sprawling, 90-acre, open-air museum is in Northern Phoenix. It's not as remote as the original location of the Flying V Cabin, but you will definitely feel the pioneer experience, including some unspoiled vistas of the desert hills, flora, and fauna. The Flying V Cabin was at an elevation higher than where the saguaro cactus thrives, so imagine it with ash, cottonwood, and pine trees.

Among the original structures there are other pioneer homes, a schoolhouse, and an opera house known as Howey Hall. Some of the reconstructed buildings include a sheriff's office, a blacksmith, a bank, and a church, and there's a Museum of Telephone History, chronicling the early days of telegraph and telephone communications. If you come here to escape the hustle and bustle of the city, check out the cabin first and then explore the rest of this fascinating museum that feels frozen in time.

Address 3901 W Pioneer Road, Phoenix, AZ 85086, +1 (623) 465-1052, www.pioneeraz.org, info@pioneeraz.org | Getting there By car, take I-17 north to exit 225 to W Pioneer Road | Hours Daily 9am–4pm | Tip For a fun-filled family adventure – no family feuding – bring the kids to the Children's Museum of Phoenix, open seven days a week (215 N 7th Street, www.childrensmuseumofphoenix.org).

38 Frank Lloyd Wright Spire

Commemorative park hidden in plain sight

Anyone who dared call this stunning landmark an "eyesore" certainly did not know that it was Frank Lloyd Wright himself who had designed this tower in 1957 for the Arizona State Capitol Annex in Papago Park. The futuristic design was rejected at that time because some thought it was *too* futuristic, but it was finally built in 2004, 45 years after Wright passed away in Phoenix.

Located at the southeast corner of Scottsdale Road and aptly named Frank Lloyd Wright Boulevard, this treasure towers 125 feet over a modest yet richly appointed park at The Scottsdale Promenade shopping center, hidden in plain sight. And even today, people still either adore it or don't care much for it.

The tower is illuminated day and night. During the daytime hours, translucent components let the light shine through. It is lit up via internal blue LED lights at night. The blues and greens of the spire represent turquoise and copper ores found throughout the State of Arizona, and the structure is constructed of 1,700 pieces of steel and weighs in at a whopping 75,000 pounds. Also in this pocket park is a pavilion, a reflecting pool, and numerous sculptures by Wright apprentice Heloise Crista.

Wright's unsolicited design received national media attention and split the city's enthusiasm for his concept. After the design was ultimately rejected, he went on to create the Grady Gammage Auditorium on the Arizona State University campus, which now receives more tourists than the Arizona State Capitol. When the spire was finally commissioned for construction in 2004, it was Arnold Roy, architecture apprentice to Frank Lloyd Wright at Taliesin West, who updated Wright's original design, bringing it up to today's construction codes, while retaining all of the hallmark elements of the original. Roy was also the architect of the Frank Lloyd Wright Commemorative Park, where the tower stands today.

Address Corner of N Scottsdale Road & E Frank Lloyd Wright Boulevard, Scottsdale, AZ 85254 | **Getting there** Bus 72 to Bell & Scottsdale Roads, 170 to Frank Lloyd Wright Boulevard & Scottsdale Road | **Hours** Unrestricted | **Tip** Taliesin West, the headquarters for the Frank Lloyd Wright Foundation, was Wright's winter home and his studio in the desert from 1937 until his death in 1959 (12621 N Frank Lloyd Wright Boulevard, Scottsdale, franklloydwright.org).

39__Fry Bread House

Community is the most important ingredient

Cecelia Miller, a Native American of the Tohono O'odham Nation, Sells District, launched Fry Bread House in 1992. In 2012, it won the James Beard Award as an American Classic.

The dining destination was featured on Guy Fieri's Food Network show, "Diners, Drive-Ins, and Dives." He loved it so much that he could barely talk about how delicious the fry bread dishes are between taking bites. However, the awards, the television shows, and five-star reviews are not the crown jewels of this humble establishment. Miller's vision from the very beginning was to create a place where Native Americans can come and enjoy foods that they know and love. It's a community where all are welcome.

The giant, pillowy, crunch-on-the-outside, soft-on-the-inside fry bread is Miller's own recipe. You must try the Native taco and then the honey-and-powdered-sugar fry bread for dessert. But also try the green chili stew and the *posole*. Bring your appetite. The fry bread here is big.

The art in the restaurant is a rotating gallery of the family's art collection, much of which belonged to the parents. The kids were raised with an appreciation for all the arts, including painting, stage, and music. Speaking of art, the restaurant hosts two vendors per day, most of whom are friends of the family and known in the local Native American community.

After Cecelia passed away in 2020, her children Jennifer and Richard stepped forward to continue the business. So even after more than 30 years in business, it's still family owned and run, and all the siblings have had a hand in continuing Cecelia's legacy. Jennifer is planning for the future, too. While honoring her mother's vision and their cultural heritage, she wants to add some healthier options to the menu and hopes one day to expand the size of the restaurant so that they can host special and milestone events for the community.

Address 4545 N 7th Avenue, Phoenix, AZ 85013, +1 (602) 351-2345, www.frybreadhouseaz.com, frybreadhouseaz@gmail.com | Getting there Bus 8 to 7th & W Campbell Avenues | Hours Mon–Sat 11am–8pm | Tip A short distance north is Belly Melrose, a tiny, two-story restaurant bursting with Vietnamese, Thai, and Japanese flavors. Great for a date night! (4971 N 7th Avenue, www.bellyphx.com/melrose/belly-melrose-home).

40 Fry's Downtown

Construction revealed recent and ancient history

When Fry's Food & Drug opened in 2019 at 1st and Jefferson Streets downtown, it ended a decades-long food desert. But it also revealed secrets of Phoenix's past.

In the store's two-story atrium, look for a portion of a brick wall that has been given a lofty display. Most people don't even notice it, but this brick wall is from Phoenix's first fire station, which once stood on this historic site. The sizable section of original bricks is adorned with a large, black, metal Phoenix Fire Department logo and is covered with a clear sheet of acrylic for protection. But the locale's history goes much farther back.

Not long ago, this block, Block 23 of the city site's original numbered block system, was the home of the 1931 Fox Theatre movie palace (closed in 1975) and a 1953 "ultra-modern" J. C. Penny's department store, both long since razed. And before that, the site hosted Phoenix's first fire station and city hall. The first, all-volunteer Phoenix fire department was organized in 1886 and started with 25 men, but it wouldn't be until 1894 that the first brick-and-mortar fire station would be built here. The impressive, two-story station had four bay doors and a 1,222-pound alarm bell, which later was moved to City Hall because of structural support issues. City Hall has moved at least twice since. You can see the bell at the Phoenix Fire Department Administration building.

It's rare that archeologists have the opportunity to "dig" amongst skyscrapers, but they had such a chance during excavation for today's downtown Fry's. They found artifacts from two fire stations, built in 1894 and 1915, as well as artifacts predating the Hohokam Indians, the civilization that built the canal system. From the sidewalk on 1st Street and looking into the café inside, you can see large format historic photographs of Phoenix's first fire station, including one with a gathering of Phoenix's first firefighters.

Address 100 E Jefferson Street, Phoenix, AZ 85004, www.frysfood.com | Getting there Valley Metro Light Rail to Washington/Central Avenue, Jefferson/1st Avenue, or 3rd Street/Jefferson | Hours Daily 6am–11pm | Tip The Sunday morning Downtown Phoenix Farmers Market features dozens of vendors offering seasonally grown, local foods and products, alongside several food trucks (720 N 5th Street, www.downtownphoenixfarmersmarket.org/this-saturday-at-the-market).

41 GenuWine Arizona

Enjoy self-pour wines from Arizona

While on vacation in France, former 7th grade math teacher Emily Rieve texted her friend and former 7th grade science teacher Lindsey Schoenemann. Rieve was very excited about her discovery of self-pour technology. And she had an idea that she wanted to share with her friend right away. She suggested that the two ladies open a self-pour wine shop. Lindsey's initial reaction was, "You're crazy."

But the notion took flight, and in January 2018, a mere 14 months later, GenuWine opened its doors in downtown Phoenix on the super-popular Roosevelt Row. Both business owners were originally from small towns in the Midwest and knew that they wanted to offer a community vibe because "atmosphere" was of the utmost importance. That's exactly what they have delivered in this comfortable space that features and promotes local wine, art, and foods.

The self-pour wall features 24 bottles of wine. The local wines are marked with a star, and each guest may select a 1, 3, or 5-ounce self-pour. There are tasting notes near each bottle featured in the well-lit, transparent boxes. GenuWine also is a bottle shop, so when you taste a wine you like, you can buy a bottle (or two) to go. Look for the "Arizona Wines" wall for your new favorite local wine. They also have six taps offering local beers. The local wines and beers change frequently, so visiting on a regular basis can be a new experience every time. Hungry, too? Check out their menu and ask about their bottle-and-board offerings.

What some would call "special events," the activities calendar here feels more like a couple of great friends are inviting you out for an evening of fun, such as a round of trivia, a game of euchre, a book club, some live music, or just hanging out and tasting wines on a Saturday night. All of those are genuine events at GenuWine, offered weekly or monthly. The wine tasting events are twice monthly, and some of them focus on a region and/or particular variety of wine.

Address 888 N 1st Avenue, Suite 101, Phoenix, AZ 85003, +1 (602) 682-7494, www.genuwinearizona.com, GenuWineAZ@gmail.com | Getting there Valley Metro Light Rail to Roosevelt/Central Avenue; bus 0 to 1st Avenue & Roosevelt Street | Hours Mon–Thu 11am–10pm, Fri & Sat 11am–11pm, Sun 11am–9pm | Tip Also woman-owned and right around the corner, Fair Trade Café offers locally roasted coffees and a delicious menu. They're the longest-standing coffee shop in downtown Phoenix (1020 N 1st Avenue, www.azfairtrade.com).

42 — Geographical Center of Phoenix

A phoenix marks the heart of Phoenix

Most locals know that the center of Phoenix is at the intersection of Central Avenue and Washington Street. Though not often discussed these days, the catastrophic flood of 1891 disrupted stagecoaches, damaged railroads, and destroyed businesses and homes. It wiped out much of budding South Phoenix, thus interrupting the city's outward growth pattern. As a result, the city sprawled north of downtown largely because of that historic catastrophic event.

However, halfway between Washington and Jefferson Streets on S Central Avenue is a massive but subtle, etched medallion that now marks the "Geographical Center of Phoenix, Arizona," as it is noted in Google Maps. Unless you glance down, you just might walk right over it. It's situated in the heart of CityScape, the location of the former Patriots Square Park, a two-block, high-rise, mixed-use development that is home to residential, retail, office, and hotel components, including some excellent dining options, live music, a comedy club, a splash pad, and the Downtown Phoenix Information Center. Interestingly, there has been little fanfare about this marker.

This area is now pedestrian-only. It will also be home to a future Valley Metro Light Rail station, part of the transportation system's South Central Extension that will travel south on Central Avenue for five miles to Baseline Road, toward South Mountain.

The medallion itself bears the image of a stylized phoenix. The mythical bird has been the city's official symbol since 1987, the result of a design campaign in which the city selected 10 finalists from 277 entries from as far away as England. Following a vote put to the public, the winning design that is the beloved and ubiquitous symbol of the city was created by the company Smit Ghormley Sanft, which later became Smit Ghormley Lofgreen.

Address West side of S Central Avenue between W Washington & W Jefferson Streets, Phoenix, AZ 85004 | Getting there Valley Metro Light Rail to Washington / Central Avenue | Hours Unrestricted | Tip While you're in CityScape, enjoy a margarita on the patio at Chico Malo. They have the best *elote* (Mexican Street Corn, served off-cobb) in town (50 W Jefferson Street, www.chicomalo.com/phoenix).

43 Giant Golden Panda

Pandas are so cute, even at 13 feet tall

Have you ever seen a giant panda up close? Have you ever seen a truly *giant* giant panda? The latter is what Phoenix has to offer, and it just might be the next best thing to seeing one of these playful, adorable creatures in real life.

In 1996, *Maternal Love*, a 13-by-13-foot bronze sculpture of a stylized giant panda cradling her cub, was gifted to the City of Phoenix from its Sister City of Chengdu, China and Mr. Wang Rongxuan, then mayor of the People's Government of Sichuan Province, Chengdu City. Around 75 percent of the world's wild giant pandas live in Sichuan Province. No longer on the endangered species list thanks to extraordinary conservation efforts, giant pandas continue to live in zoos around the world for education and breeding purposes.

The golden *Maternal Love* sculpture looks truly gigantic as it towers over its human spectators. It's situated in Margaret T. Hance Park, named for the first woman to become mayor of Phoenix. She held office for four consecutive two-year terms from 1976 to 1984. The sculpture rests in a quiet space not visible from major thoroughfares. You will want to make a point of coming to the park specifically to see it because it's so striking – and so big.

This beautiful sculpture, valued at $200,000 in 1976, was created in China and shipped to the United States. Phoenix built the platform on which it sits and paid for the shipping costs. Placement in Margaret T. Hance Park was purposeful. Phoenix has 11 Sister Cities, including Chengdu. At least three of them are represented in this same park, including Himeji, Japan; Ennis, Ireland; and Chengdu, China, with its golden panda.

The Sister Cities program, proposed in 1956 by President Dwight D. Eisenhower as a people-to-people program, today boasts participation by approximately 140 countries, with more than 1,800 foreign cities, plus every state in the United States.

Address 200 E Moreland Street, Phoenix, AZ 85004, www.phoenix.gov/parks/parks/alphabetical/h-parks/hance | Getting there Valley Metro Light Rail north to Roosevelt/Central Avenue or McDowell/Central Avenue; bus 514, 521, 522, 531, 533 to 3rd & Moreland Streets | Hours Unrestricted | Tip Now that you've seen a bear, head over to the Phoenix Zoo to see lions and tigers, too. You can see and learn about more than 3,000 animals representing nearly 400 species, some of which are threatened or endangered (455 N Galvin Parkway, www.phoenixzoo.org).

44 Giving Tree Café

"Welcome to a Space of Love"

"A Space of Love" is written on the spacious floor as you enter this delicious, organic, vegan, gluten-free café, which opened in 2019. When you arrive at the Giving Tree Café, you immediately feel serene and cared for. When you see and taste the food, you're going to feel loved. Care, purpose, and decades of experience go into every delicious drink, main course, and dessert here. Chef David Warr has lived meat-free deliciously for decades.

You may have heard the expression, "Life is short, eat dessert first." It certainly applies here, as Giving Tree is on-point with their deserts. Because they use processed-free sugar, their desserts are vegan, as well. Some do not realize that the typical five-pound bags of white sugar that they're using at home are not at all vegan. To make sugar white, it's processed with animal bone char, thus making it a non-vegan food. But not to worry. Giving Tree has taken care of those details for you so that you can truly and safely enjoy a wholly vegan meal. Due to the fact that they are not serving meat or fish, they are left with the challenge of creating alluring, appealing, and appetizing dishes. And that's one of the delights of eating at a vegetarian or vegan establishment. Giving Tree wholeheartedly accepts this challenge and takes it to the next level making their dishes absolutely beautiful, too. The appetizers and entrées are high-vibe, amazing, comfort food – no pretensions here.

No matter the time of day you go, there's a phenomenal beverage awaiting you. On the menu is a wide range of coffees: a latte or an espresso con panna; some bright lunchtime options like ginger lemonade and Super Food Soda; and for those who are hungry and simultaneously wanting to treat a sweet tooth, a Butterfingery Shake or a Mango Lassi. Then there are the visually stunning mocktails, like Lotuswei Flower Elixir and a Blue Dreamteani. They also offer events, live music, and tastings.

Address 2024 N 7th Street, #111, Phoenix, AZ 85006, +1 (480) 630-0200, www.givingtreecafe.com, givingtreecafephx@gmail.com | Getting there Bus 7 to 7th Street & Palm Lane | Hours Daily 10:30am – 9pm | Tip What could be a stand-alone sculpture is the sign for The Giving Tree Café on the north side. It's a reimagined sculpture of the famous New York City photograph *Lunch Atop a Skyscraper*, but this one features copper makers, and some of the workers are Native American. A seven-foot tall Rosie the Riveter is in on the fun (2024 N 7th Street).

45 Governor Hunt's Tomb

Arizona's first governor interred under a pyramid

Located in the southeast corner of Papago Park is a bright white, Egyptian-style pyramid atop a hill. This is the final resting place of Arizona's first governor, George W. P. Hunt (1859–1934), his wife Duett, their only child, and four other members of their extended family. In total, there are seven people buried in Hunt's tomb.

Hunt built this unique mausoleum for his wife's burial in 1931 because they had both been impressed by the Egyptian pyramids during their international travels together. The governor himself was interred here in 1934. He was 75. In addition to the governor and his wife, family members entombed in the pyramid include: their daughter Virginia, who passed in1985 at the age of 79, and her second husband William E. Frund; Mrs. Hunt's parents Jessie and Susan Ellison; and Mrs. Hunt's sister, Lena Ellison. In the governor's 1929 will, he stated, "…I want to be buried that I may in my spirit overlook this splendid valley that in the years to come will be the mecca for those that love beautiful things and in the state where the people rule."

Hunt had said that he wished he could have served in the US Marine Corps when the country entered World War I. He took up knitting scarves for those in uniform as part of his patriotic duty. A supporter of women's rights, Hunt reportedly allowed women to vote in Arizona eight years before it was legalized in the rest of the states.

In a 1911 *Graham Guardian* article, Hunt was compared to Abraham Lincoln for his "uncouth appearance and uncultured mind" and simultaneously praised as one of the greatest politicians ever known in Arizona. He also was a delegate to the Democratic National Convention in 1900 and presided over the 1910 Arizona Constitutional Convention that led to statehood in 1912. Hunt served as the state's first, second, third, sixth, seventh, eighth, and tenth governor.

Address 625 N Galvin Parkway, Phoenix, AZ 85008 | Getting there Bus 3 or 56 to Van Buren Street & Galvin Parkway, walk four blocks east to destination | Hours Daily 6am–7pm | Tip The next time you pass the upside-down Pyramid Building on Central Avenue in Midtown Phoenix, stop and take a good look at it because its structure is quite fascinating (3507 N Central Avenue, www.getyourphx.com/the-pyramid-building).

46 Grunow Memorial Clinic
Only historic building to retain its original use

The first medical clinic in the Southwest, and cited today as the only historic building in Phoenix to retain its original use, is the 1931 Lois Grunow Memorial Clinic. Its name is etched in stone above the main entrance on McDowell Road, though it's now known as Grunow Memorial Medical Center. It is the namesake of Lois Anita Grunow, a seven-year-old who died of a ruptured appendix in 1929. Her condition had been misdiagnosed. The Grunows envisioned that exceptional medical research and an outstanding medical facility might prevent fates similar to their daughter's.

The building is of Spanish Colonial Revival architecture designed by Lester Byron and a nod to missions in California. The elaborate entrance is adorned with bas-relief carvings, including some representing the medical profession. On the east front façade, you will find the immortal name "Lister," memorializing scientist Joseph Lister, who discovered a way to prevent infection in wounds during, and after, surgery, processes that we continue to employ today. On the west front facade of the building is carved "Pasteur," acknowledging scientist Louis Pasteur, who developed the food preparation process we know today as pasteurization. He also developed vaccinations for anthrax and rabies. Above the double-arch west wing entrance is carved "Laboratory Department." Inside the elaborate entrance is Memorial Hall, a beautifully designed, two-story lobby adorned with four highly placed murals that depict significant moments in medical history.

William C. Grunow was the president of Chicago's Grigsby-Grunow Company, producer of the popular Majestic radio. He quickly became a multimillionaire. He purchased his Camelback Mountain-adjacent 11-room home in 1930, soon after announcing "the establishment and operation of a great medical center in Phoenix." He and his wife Valborg Grunow, set aside an endowment of $1,000,000 for the Lois Grunow Memorial Clinic.

Address 926 E McDowell Road, Phoenix, AZ 85006 | Getting there Bus 17 to McDowell Road & 10th Street | Hours Unrestricted from outside | Tip One block east is the tower of the former Good Samaritan Hospital, built in 1978 and designed by Bertrand Goldberg, the architect best known for the Marina City complex in Chicago (1111 E McDowell Road).

47 Hanny's Bathroom
The most Instagrammable loo in town

You may know Hanny's, but did you know that the unisex restrooms upstairs used to be dressing rooms? You won't find many photographs from the space's department store days, but you will find quite a few diners in the restroom today, freshening up and taking selfies in their #OOTD (outfit of the day) amidst the flattering, Instagram-worthy, neon pink lights and lots of mirrors.

If you don't look upwards, you might miss Hanny's magnificent architecture both inside and outside, much of which has been preserved. Hanny's, a historic building, originally opened as a men's department store (hence the dressing rooms), where gentlemen shopped for the latest fashions. When the store opened in November 1947, thousands of people attended the event. Designed by the lauded firm Lescher & Mahoney, this building was a departure from the architecture in downtown Phoenix, as reported in the *Arizona Times*. Its International-style design had become popular in the US in the 1930s but did not reach Phoenix until the 1940s. This building is one of the few examples of such architecture remaining in Phoenix.

Hanny's restaurant and bar opened in 2005, repurposing some key features of the original building. Test your acrophobia as you peer down the old elevator shaft. No need to worry about falling, though, as it's covered with thick, clear acrylic for your viewing pleasure. And you can't miss the fanciful art installations in the restaurant, some of which you can see from the sidewalk. Hanny's is also a great destination for a late-night cocktail.

The seating options here are all good. There is mezzanine seating, bar seating, standard tables, and some wonderful, window-facing group seating. Head downstairs to the basement to find a collection of antique dolls, both creepy and fascinating. The restaurant offers a "Dinner with the Dolls" experience for those who dare.

Address 40 N 1st Street, Phoenix, AZ 85004, +1 (602) 252-2285, www.hannys.net |
Getting there Valley Metro Light Rail to Washington/Central Avenue | Hours Sat–Mon
5pm–1am, Tue–Fri 11:30–1am | Tip You definitely want to go to the bathroom when
visiting OdySea. When you're washing your hands at the sink, instead of a mirror you
have a window that looks directly into the shark tank (9500 E Via de Ventura, Scottsdale,
www.odyseaaquarium.com).

48__Hawk Salvage

Your destination for one-of-a-kind curios

"Amazing items from across the globe. Interesting, Rare, Unique, Collection of cool stuff." That's a direct marketing quote for Hawk Salvage, but no words can quite capture the true essence of the collections curated by Greg Hawk (also known as "Hawk"), founder, owner, and enthusiastic treasure hunter. The unique items here could only be found by someone like Hawk, who himself is one of a kind, who scouts for objects he himself finds interesting and that also appeal to people of discerning taste.

Here, you may find a collection of 1800s prosthetic eyeballs; Ex Libris prints from Eastern Europe with provenance; an antique leather dentist chair; dozens of anatomical, hand-painted lithographs from the Netherlands circa 1800s, one of only three known sets of its kind in the world; and a collection of 1950s coasters of the erotica genre penned by a customer in a bar in the Netherlands. That's just the tip of the iceberg.

And did you know that Arizona has an "official" State Neckwear? It's, of course, the bola tie. Hawk Salvage has many to choose from, as well as a lot of other curious, interesting, and thought-provoking jewelry, including a vast collection of hat and lapel pins. The curios here range from erotica, death, occult, and anatomy, to live plants and "weird" collectibles.

A former captain with Phoenix Fire Department, Hawk began collecting around 2006, started selling at antique markets around 2010, and in 2019 purchased his gallery building on Grand Avenue, a hub for burgeoning and experimental artists, and the original site of First Fridays in Phoenix. The exterior is sparsely but smartly adorned. You'll find the garage door open during events, while the back part of the gallery is used for art shows, interactive art demonstrations, and the occasional fashion show, often including food trucks and live music.

Address 1109 Grand Avenue, Phoenix, AZ 85007, +1 (602) 790-8365, www.instagram.com/hawksalvage | Getting there Bus 3 to Van Buren Street & 7th Avenue, bus 15 to 15th Avenue & Roosevelt Street | Hours Thu, Fri & Sat, call for opening hours; see Instagram for special events | Tip Only steps away, check out the award-winning Grand Avenue Brewing Company, featuring unfiltered, "bottle conditioned" beers (1205 W Pierce Street, www.grandavebrew.com).

49 _Her Secret is Patience_
Inspired by monsoon clouds

Something ethereal is hovering 145 feet above Civic Space Park in downtown Phoenix. Is it a UFO, an elongated dreamcatcher, or perhaps a tornado? Those are some of the postulations of passersby. Artist Janet Echelman is known for building "sculptural interventions that respond to environmental forces" like wind and water, or in the case of _Her Secret is Patience_, Arizona's monsoon clouds, saguaro flower, and saguaro boots, which are bird nests inside a saguaro cactus, often home to the cactus wren, Arizona's State Bird.

The name for Civic Space Park's centerpiece comes from advice of American poet, essayist, and philosopher Ralph Waldo Emerson, who wrote, "Adopt the pace of nature: her secret is patience." It serves as a reminder "that life shouldn't be consumed by impatience, and that adopting nature's pace requires patience and empathy for oneself and others. It can also encourage people to slow down, observe the beauty of everyday life, and embrace the natural world," according to the Poetry Foundation.

The best time to see this magnificent work is after sunset, against the background of the night sky. You can see it if you're riding Valley Metro light rail traveling either north (Van Buren/Central Ave Station) or south (after the McDowell/Central Ave Station). It feels like an interactive sculpture as you walk past, as it waves delicately with even the slightest breeze. From directly underneath it, you can see through to the sky.

One of the aspects that awarded Echelman the coveted contract for this project was its massive size without encroaching on the limited space of this modest 2.7-acre park. Completed in 2009, _Her Secret is Patience_ is credited with playing a crucial role in the revitalization of downtown Phoenix. The work is a permanent piece in the city's public art program, so it will be here today and for generations to come.

Address 424 N Central Avenue, Phoenix, AZ 85004, www.echelman.com | **Getting there** Valley Metro Light Rail to Van Buren / Central Avenue or Van Buren / 1st Avenue; bus 0, 8 to Central Avenue & ASU University Center | **Hours** Unrestricted | **Tip** Continue your skyward experience with a visit to the Dorrance Planetarium at the Arizona Science Center (600 E Washington Street, www.azscience.org/attractions/dorrance-planetarium).

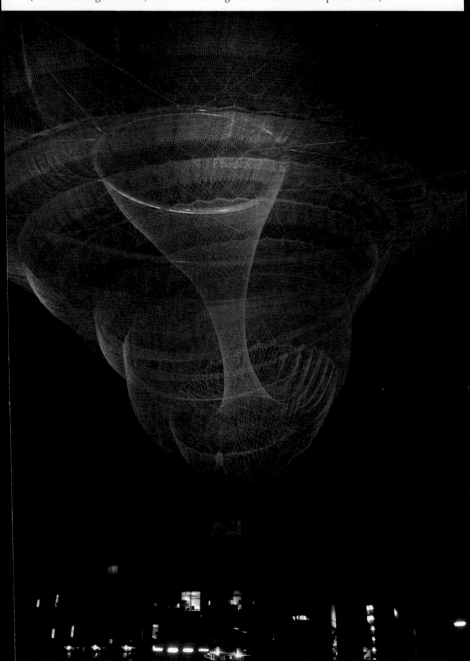

50 Historic Fire Station 8

If the engine is in the driveway, they're open

"Prevent harm. Survive. Be nice." That's the motto of the Phoenix Fire Department, and it's prominently displayed throughout Historic Fire Station 8 in Willo Historic Neighborhood, one of the first and largest historic districts in Phoenix.

Planned in the 1920s, Willo is just northwest of downtown, yet close enough that now it is part of Central Phoenix. Willo has more than 700 homes, all built primarily in the first half of the 20th century in a wide variety of styles. Built in 1942, the Mission Revival-style Fire Station 8 was originally a private home.

While not credentialed as a museum, this historic fire station has museum-quality artifacts, including uniforms, helmets, trophies, plaques, ladders, alarm pulls, axes, and other fire-fighting equipment. The layout of the structure is close to its original configuration. A sign that reads "Poop Deck" leads to the station's communications room. They also have on display the turnout jacket that belonged to Margaret T. Hance (1923–1990), Phoenix's first female mayor.

The photograph collection here chronicles Phoenix Fire Department history from its very beginning. There are images of fire stations, firefighting activity, firefighter life, as well as photos of legendary, pioneering, and fallen firefighter heroes and their "last alarm." Also look for cases of other artifacts and a toy dalmation.

The jewel of the station is its antique fire engine. This 1941 Chevrolet Fire Engine Pumper is one of only about 1,000 ever made, noted by Tim Kovacs, who has an illustrious career with the fire department. Today, one of his favorite responsibilities with the Phoenix Fire Department is being the trusted steward and host for tours of Historic Fire Station 8. The station was in service until 1978, when it became a Battalion Office. There's another gem of an automobile here: a pristine, mint-condition 1978 Dodge Monaco that was once owned by a former Fire Battalion chief.

Address 541 W Encanto Boulevard, Phoenix, AZ 85003, www.facebook.com/ PhoenixFireHistoricStation8, PFDHxFS08@gmail.com | **Getting there** Bus 8 to 7th Avenue & Encanto Boulevard | **Hours** Look for a fire engine outside or email for tour request | **Tip** Visit the Firefighter Bell Tower, a memorial to fallen volunteer Phoenix firefighters erected in 1910 at Greenwood Memory Lawn (719 N 27th Avenue).

51 Historic Sahuaro Ranch

Peacocks with ties to Chicago and Mexico

While "beauty is in the eye of the beholder," most people would agree that peacocks are among the most beautiful animals in the world. The dozens of stunning peafowl at Historic Sahuaro Ranch are one of the many aspects of Arizona settler life you will discover here. Peacocks are known more for their extravagant plumage used in courting rituals with the more modest peahens than for their practical nature, but farmers have long used them for insect and pest control. And they eat snakes, too. Peafowl typically live in forests, grasslands, open woodlands, and, in this case, on a historic ranch.

The ranch was founded after the completion of the Arizona Canal in 1885, before Glendale was a city, by William Bartlett, who homesteaded the ranch in 1886 and continued until his death in 1918. Bartlett outsourced the management of the ranch, only living here for approximately six months.

The ranch had draft horses and mules, as well as cows, bulls, and hogs. On the crop front, there were figs, vineyards, and fields of alfalfa for the livestock. In the early days, there was a 100-acre olive orchard and a 20-acre orange grove, both among the first to be grown in the valley. Arizona would become a significant region for citrus and olive groves. There are still big, lush olive trees and a small orchard of orange trees here.

In 1927, Richard W. Smith purchased the ranch and built many of the more than 15 historic buildings that you see today. Many years later, the City of Glendale purchased 80 of the original 640 acres with the intention of making it the park we enjoy today, which is listed on the National Register of Historical Places. The Historic Main House contains many of the original furnishings, including the family's Victrola record player, a radio, and a full bedroom set on the second floor. Stop and smell the flowers in the lovely rose garden in front of the house before you come indoors.

Address 9802 N 59th Avenue, Glendale, AZ 85302, www.glendaleaz.com/Live/Amenities/ parks_facilities_trails/regional_parks/sahuaro_ranch_park | Getting there Bus GUS 3, 59 to 59th Avenue & Mountain View Road | Hours Park: daily 6am–10pm; historic areas: daily dawn–dusk | Tip Enjoy a two-for-one in historic downtown Glendale's Entertainment District, which includes Old Towne and Historic Catlin Court, where you'll find eateries and charming shops. Start at Murphy Park (7010 N 58th Avenue, Glendale, www.visitdowntownglendale.com).

52 Hohokam Ancestral Grounds

Meet the Native Americans who built our canals

The canals that were resurrected and used to build Phoenix were designed and constructed by the Hohokam Indians. Some have said that the Hohokam disappeared, and it's now considered an ancient civilization, but that's not entirely true. One of the many things you will discover when visiting S'edav Va'aki Museum is that the Hohokam are the ancestors of today's Tohono O'odham Nation. Some Hohokam villages – you're standing in one when you visit the museum – were continuously occupied for 1,500 years. The incredibly complex canal system was originally built by the engineers of the era between 600 and 1450 B.C.E. The Hohokam mysteriously left the area that is present-day Phoenix, but it's theorized that there was a sustained drought, and the Hohokam followed fertile grounds.

The City of Phoenix, referencing the mythological bird that is reborn from its own ashes, was named in honor of the Hohokam, as present day Phoenician society rose from the ingenuity and hard work of the Native Americans who came before us, the people who built the waterways that continue to sustain life in Metro Phoenix.

The S'edav Va'aki Museum, formerly Pueblo Grande, is an archaeological site and sacred grounds. The indoor museum features artifacts from the site and interpretive displays. Look for the map that shows more than 1,000 miles of canals built in the area. Also on the grounds is an adobe house compound replica, designed based on archaeological research on homelife in the Southwest. Because of modern day building codes, the ceilings of these houses are higher than the ones that would have been here from 1150 to 1450 B.C.E. Venture to the houses and explore what homelife would have been like for the Hohokam people here. The Hohokam represents one of the largest, most complex societies to ever live in the Phoenix and Tucson basins.

Address 4619 E Washington Street, Phoenix, AZ 85034, +1 (602) 495-0900, www.phoenix.gov/sedav-vaaki | Getting there Valley Metro Light Rail 44th Street/ Washington; bus 1, 32, 44 to 44th & Washington Streets | Hours See website for seasonal hours | Tip Explore the canals by walking, running, or biking along the trails (throughout Phoenix, www.srpnet.com/grid-water-management/water-recreation/canal-trails).

53 Home of the Diamondbacks

Tour Chase Field year-round

What has a refreshing swimming pool, a retractable roof, and can host more than 48,500 people? That would be Chase Field, home of the Arizona Diamondbacks, the 2001 World Series champions, a feat this expansion team accomplished a mere four seasons after their debut.

Tours of Chase Field are available year-round, except when the D-backs have a day-game, there's a special event, or it happens to be a major holiday. Chase Field was the first stadium built in the US with a retractable roof over a natural grass field. Although it has used artificial turf since 2019, the retractable roof remains open until temperatures reach above 100 degrees Fahrenheit.

You enter the stadium at Gate E, where standard security procedures are in place. You will tour the various levels of the stadium and venture underground to see where all the pre-game magic happens. Some of the destinations include: the press booth, luxurious guest suites, and the media room where televised interviews take place, and one of the only swimming pools in a baseball stadium, this one offered as a suite. The stadium features nearly a quarter mile of concession stands. If you're there for a game, look for Arizona Street Tacos on one of the upper floors. You will also learn why our mascot is a bobcat named Baxter instead of a diamondback rattlesnake.

Throughout the stadium are historic photographs of baseball legends, including Joe DiMaggio and Babe Ruth, as well as poster-sized photos of celebrities who have performed at Chase Field including Pink, Black Sabbath, Kenny Chesney, NSYNC, and Sir Elton John. Walking around the sea of green chairs, you will hear the story about the single red chair in the stadium. It's never sold for a game, not even during the World Series. The grand finale of the tour is a visit to the Diamondbacks' dugout.

Address 401 E Jefferson Street, Phoenix, AZ 85004, +1 (602) 462-6799, www.mlb.com/dbacks/ballpark/tours, ballparktours@dbacks.com | **Getting there** Valley Metro Light Rail to 3rd Street / Jefferson; bus 1, SME, SR 51 to Jefferson & 7th Streets | **Hours** Tours Mon–Sat 9:30am, 11am, 12:30pm | **Tip** A few steps away at Footprint Center, shop for all things basketball at the Phoenix Suns and Phoenix Mercury Team Shop (201 E Jefferson Street, www.shop.suns.com).

54 Ira H. Hayes USMC Memorial

Pima Indian was one of the Iwo Jima flag raisers

Ira Hamilton Hayes (1923–1955), a Native American from nearby Gila River Indian Community, was one of the six Marines who raised the American flag at Iwo Jima on Friday, February 23, 1945. Captured in Joe Rosenthal's (1911–2006) Pulitzer Prize-winning photograph, the scene is depicted in the design of the US Marine Corps War Memorial in Arlington, Virginia, near Arlington National Cemetery, where Hayes is buried.

The Ira H. Hayes USMC Memorial is located in the Matthew B. Juan – Ira H. Hayes Veterans Memorial Park in the Sacaton District, the capital of Gila River Indian Community, where the tribal administrative offices and departments are located. Matthew B. Juan, raised in Sacaton, was the first Native American and the first Arizonan to be killed during World War I. That was May 28, 1918, and the first American offensive operation of the war. The park also hosts a monument to Juan, dedicated in 1928.

Ira H. Hayes, born in Sacaton, was an Akimel O'odham and a decorated soldier. He was awarded the Bronze Star before his deployment to Iwo Jima. Accounts from friends and family say that Hayes was humble and hardworking, and a happy person. He was, however, born only one generation after the Akimel O'odham, or Pima, people suffered a "terrible famine" on the Gila River reservation. Dams upriver cut off water to the reservation, devastating its once flourishing agricultural culture, wiping away the engineering marvel of the canals they had built by hand to irrigate their bountiful farmlands.

The park is home to numerous memorials, including a bronze statue of both soldiers. The one of Hayes, sculpted by a fellow Native American Pima, was erected in 1992 by the Ira H. Hayes American Legion Post 84.

Address 145 W Casa Blanca Road, Sacaton, AZ 85147, www.irahayespost84.org/index.php |
Getting there By car, take I-10 to exit 175 to Casa Blanca Road and drive southeast to
destination | Hours Unrestricted | Tip Stay on the reservation and enjoy an afternoon or
evening, or longer, at the popular Sheraton Grand at Wild Horse Pass (5594 W Wild Horse
Pass Boulevard, Chandler, www.wildhorsepassresort.com).

55 Irish Cultural Center

A tale of a collection, a cottage, and a castle

You can fully immerse yourself in Irish culture – beyond a pint of Guinness and an annual St. Patrick's Day Parade – at the Irish Cultural Center and McClelland Library in downtown Phoenix. This campus is home to a memorial, an 1850s cottage, a great hall, a castle, and relics, including a very large, iron famine pot. Honoring Ireland's cultural heritage, the Center preserves, teaches, and engages fellow Irish and all others interested in the country's rich, storied, and accomplished history.

It was on St. Patrick's Day in 1988 that Ennis in County Clare, Ireland, an area of the Emerald Isle near the North Atlantic Ocean, became Phoenix's fifth Sister City. Some early Phoenix and Arizona settlers of Irish descent brought with them the Luck of the Irish, but most worked hard and determinedly, and some became famous. One lucky native of Ireland was William "Buckey" O'Neill (1860–1898). He arrived in Phoenix in 1879 and became the first editor of the *Phoenix Gazette*, among many other roles throughout his life.

You will discover vast amounts of Irish history inside the castle that houses the McClelland Library on the first level. Upstairs is a genealogy room, where you can research your own Irish connections. The Rare Books Room is elegant, and its fireplace is appointed with tiles from Ireland. On the third floor, you'll find the embattled parapet walls that you see from the street. A truly beautiful castle, it fortifies the history of Irish Arizonans and beyond.

On a guided tour, you get to explore a replica Bunratty cottage which reveals what close quarters were like for families in the mid-19th century. Period furnishings and artifacts from Ireland proudly adorn the cottage. You will notice the barn-like Great Hall, where you can attend movie nights, cultural events, and Irish dances. The Irish Cultural Center is a local treasure, practically hidden in plain sight, and a pot of gold in downtown Phoenix.

Address 1106 N Central Avenue, Phoenix, AZ 85004, +1 (602) 258-0109, www.azirish.org, info@azirish.org | Getting there Valley Metro Light Rail to Roosevelt/Central Avenue; bus 0 to Central Avenue & Roosevelt Street | Hours See website for seasonal hours and events | Tip Dubliner Irish Pub & Restaurant was the first Irish pub in Phoenix and the first to pour Guinness from a tap in all the Valley of the Sun (3841 E Thunderbird Road, www.dublineririshpubaz.com).

56 Japanese Friendship Garden

Showcasing four regions of Japan

Not exactly what you would expect to find in the Sonoran Desert, the Japanese Friendship Garden in Margaret T. Hance Park hosts plants that can survive and thrive in Phoenix's harsh, hot summers. *Rohoen*, pronounced as it's spelled, is the garden's Japanese name. "Ro" is Japanese for the Heron, "Ho" is the mythological phoenix, and "En" means garden.

Arizona's first authentic Japanese garden was created with the help of master gardeners from Japan. It was, and is, a collaboration between Phoenix and Sister City Himeji, Japan. In fact, more than 50 Himeji landscape and garden architects lent their knowledge and expertise in the design of Rohoen. As you explore this 3.5-acre strolling garden, you will experience a world of tranquility, discover humble splendor, and happen upon a few surprises.

At the front and back of the garden, there are two large *shachi*, legendary sea creatures from Japanese folklore with the head of a dragon and body of a carp, protectors against fire. They are gifts from Himeji and are designed after the *shachi* at Himeji Castle, a UNESCO World Heritage Site and the last remaining wooden castle in Japan.

On the northern edge of the large, central pond is the Mayor's Tree and plaque, a spot that offers some of the best views of the garden. Installed on the occasion of the proclamation of Rohoen, the plaque has the name of every mayor of Himeji and every mayor of Phoenix inscribed on it since that time. There's also an authentic tea house, a pagoda, numerous lanterns, a 14-foot-tall waterfall, at least 50 different varieties of plant life, and 300 koi. You'll see many of them from the zig-zag bridge.

Four regions of Japan are represented in this compact treasure of a Japanese hide-and-reveal garden.

Address 1125 N 3rd Avenue, Phoenix, AZ 85003, +1 (602) 274-8700, www.japanesefriendshipgarden.org, info@jfgphx.org | Getting there Valley Metro Light Rail to Roosevelt / Central Avenue | Hours Tue–Thu 8am–noon, Fri–Sun 8am–noon & 5pm–8pm | Tip Look for lovebirds, one of the smallest parrot species, in Willo Historic Neighborhood's Walton Park, one of the city's smallest city parks (301 W Holly Street).

57 Liberty Bell

Arizona's traveled the state, and beyond

France not only gave us the Statue of Liberty, they also (for a nominal fee) created exact replicas of the Liberty Bell – one for each state and the District of Columbia – for the 1950 Independence US Savings Bond Drive. The original order was for 49, but two more were ordered with the foresight that Hawaii and Alaska might be granted statehood. Arizona's bell, now displayed near the Arizona State Capitol Museum, was displayed throughout the state before returning to Phoenix for display in the Capitol Building rotunda with plans to on a future date move it to its final display space in front of the Arizona State Capitol – today the museum – so that even more people could see it. The original Liberty Bell also had been on more than half a dozen cross-country road trips between 1885 and 1915.

The bell was unveiled at the Encanto Bandshell with remarks from Mayor Dan Edward Garvey and Hollywood movie star Richard Carlson who was in Phoenix filming *The Sound of Fury*. He also starred in *Creature from the Black Lagoon*, *It Came From Outer Space*, and *The Valley of Gwangi* – a film showing cowboys fighting a dinosaur. In Fury, at about 1:06, you'll see the Maricopa County Old Courthouse – you could drive right up to the front door where today there's a park. At the unveiling ceremonies, Carlson gave a reading based on the Declaration of Independence.

The Arizona Liberty Bell holds two unique distinctions. It was the first replica to be replicated for the bond drive and it was the only bell to have been loaned to another state during the 1950 bond drive. With only two weeks remaining in the bond drive, California had too much territory still to cover, so it borrowed the Arizona bell to tour around The Golden State, or, perhaps also apropos, The Land of Make Believe. The overall tour was a success, and the Liberty Bell remains as strong a patriotic symbol as ever.

Address 1700 W Washington Street, Phoenix, AZ 85007 | Getting there Bus 514, 521, 522, 531, 533, 535, 542, 562 to 17th Avenue & State Capitol | Hours Unrestricted | Tip Everything we know and do today started with an idea. Take the kids to the i.d.e.a. Museum and revel in their awe and brilliance (150 W Pepper Place, Mesa, www.ideamuseum.org).

58 LIX Uptown Ice Cream
Award-winning and even lactose-free

Whether it's the colorful, rooftop, inflatable unicorn, the whimsical, fun, and often surprising décor, or the hip, retro lounge in the back that intrigues you, you are certain to find a unique flavor of ice cream that resonates with your unique ice cream cravings every time you visit LIX Uptown Ice Cream.

Owner and ice cream flavor wizard Rich Dolan said, "We start every batch with the intention that it provokes a serendipitous experience in each and every guest. Only positive vibes are allowed in the kitchen when we cook and churn. In fact, we often make it a dance party." Dolan's dedication to creating phenomenal ice cream experiences is evident in his electric excitement about the shop, not to mention the ice cream cone tattoo on his forearm.

"Creamy" is an adjective often used to describe the frequently rotating ice cream flavors here, as is "delicious." And, surprisingly, it's lactose-free. Dolan painstakingly curates intriguing flavors, oftentimes a complex process. You can enjoy Ferocious Chocolate, Fig and Goat Cheese, Strawberry Quick, Biscoff Biotch, Mexican Wedding Cookie (gluten-free), Mango Sticky Rice (vegan), Turkish Coffee, and Rosemary Butter Pecan flavors, to name just a few.

If you're out enjoying a day on your own and want to have a cool treat – and it's truly a treat – you have a friend waiting for you at LIX. It could be the giant, pink gorilla on the comfy sofa in the front – a fantastic photo-op – or the friendly staff behind the counter eager to share the latest flavors with you (you can try a couple before you decide). When you've made your selection, you can ask for it in a recyclable paper cup or a chocolate-dipped waffle cone, a big one.

Come here with a date or a group of friends, or simply because you must have ice cream now. The portions are generous, and the toppings options are seemingly endless. Unicorn sprinkles, anyone?

Address 3343-3 N 7th Avenue, Phoenix, AZ 85013, +1 (602) 908-3630, https://getyourlix.com, lixuptown@gmail.com | Getting there Bus 8 to 7th Avenue & Osborn Road | Hours Mon 4–10pm, Tue–Sat noon–10pm, Sun noon–8pm | Tip Have a gastronomic celebration at Novel Ice Cream with a highly customizable, creatively fun ice cream sandwich. Think "Cookie Monster," with blue ice cream sandwiched between chocolate chip cookies and rolled in Cap'n Crunch cereal (1028 Grand Avenue #6, www.novelicecream.com).

59 __ Long Wong's

Deliciously "winging it" since 1980

What do the Statue of Liberty, a funky sleeve of French fries, a golden gorilla, several dinosaurs, and a baby giraffe have in common? Evidently, they all like chicken wings. Long Wong's on Thomas Road is home to a colorful menagerie of characters greeting all chicken wing lovers. Some of the beasties wield banners announcing, "Do wings, not drugs," "I'm in the mood for wings," and "I shoulda ate at Long Wong's." And you can immortalize your visit with a photo in the Long Wong's VW Love Bug, spray-painted in the spirited colors of the 1970s.

Heather, a local fan of Long Wong's, shared, "Steven Ashbrook, a local singer who started out at Long Wong's, has an album titled 'Live at Long Wong's.' He's great." Ashbrook, a resident of Phoenix, has won *The Phoenix Tribune*'s Best Acoustic Performer award (in Tempe), and he's played for President Bill Clinton at the request of the White House.

Driving down Thomas Road, you can't help but do a double-take at the brightly colored front "lawn" of Long Wong's and wonder what it must be. As the brain begins to process the purpose of this eclectic, electric display, with bright red letters on a bright yellow background that spell out "WINGS," you'll come to your own conclusion that it must be a hot wings restaurant – and a fun one at that. As you can imagine, the interior follows suit with its multifarious collection of tchotchkes, but on a considerably smaller scale.

You must have the chicken wings, but also enjoy the burgers, fries, and onion rings, and they also have a hotdog called the Long Wong, of course. Not to be missed on their menu is their Two-Hippies 'Magic' Brownie – teasing those who have enjoyed certain herbs legal in Arizona since the early 2020s. The dessert comes with a disclaimer, "Availability may vary. Contains 0-percent THC…it's just a really good chocolate brownie."

Address 2812 E Thomas Road, Phoenix, AZ 85016, +1 (602) 224-5464,
www.longwongs28st.com | **Getting there** Bus 29 to Thomas Road & 28th Street | **Hours**
Daily 10am–10pm | **Tip** Located in the historic, 1885 Fry Building, Majerle's Sports Grill
is the place to watch a game. Named for Phoenix Suns legend Dan Majerle, this sports
bar has approximately a bazillion TV screens and excellent bar food (24 N 2nd Street,
www.majerles.com).

60 MacAlpine's Soda Fountain

Ice cream sundaes, dinner with pie, and antiques

Driving by, you automatically know this place is historic just from the retro signage for "MacAlpine's Diner & Soda Fountain," which is exactly what you find inside. You're greeted at the door by a tall case of homemade pies with a note indicating that they're made from Amish recipes. The bright marquee lights, green barstools trimmed in chrome, a mirrored back wall, and countertop jukeboxes welcome you to this 1929 soda fountain. The soda jerks are very friendly and ready to give you a classic, retro diner experience.

If you sit at the soda fountain counter, your server will make your ice cream sundae, ice cream float, or milkshake right in front of you. Pie à la mode is a local favorite. The pie flavors vary regularly, but the Naughty Pecan Pie is a favorite. It has a buttery crust and is topped with a generous layer of caramel. You can also sit in one of the comfy wooden booths with family and friends. The wall décor is retro eclectic, but it's presented in a cohesive theme that fully captures what MacAlpine's is: a place where friends gather for a fun time. Many have enjoyed time here including Joan Ganz Cooney, one of the creators of *Sesame Street*.

At the beginning of the COVID-19 pandemic in 2020, this beloved destination closed its doors. Owner Cary Heizenrader dreamed of reopening the café. Sadly, he passed away during the years of closure, but his wife Monica reopened the restaurant in 2024, with an outpouring of support from longtime, devoted, ice-cream-sundae-loving customers.

Immediately next door, you will find another of the owner's businesses, an antique shop, which you can also access via an entry inside the café itself. It's loaded with vintage goodies and offers practically infinite flashbacks to the good ol' days. MacAlpine's is one of the very few remaining original soda fountains in the United States.

Address 2303 N 7th Street, Phoenix, AZ 85006, +1 (602) 262-5545, www.macalpines.com, macalpinesdiner@gmail.com | Getting there Bus 7 to N 7th & Oak Streets | Hours See website for current hours | Tip Enjoy more vintage vibes at Welcome Diner, circa 1945, where you can enjoy retro fare with a Southern influence, like biscuits and gravy or chicken fried steak (929 E Pierce Street, www.welcomediner.net).

61 *Magic Carpet* Underpass
Taking beautification to great heights

If you've ever dreamed of riding on a magic carpet, you're in luck! Well, it's more like a lovely walk along a pedestrian passageway under E Camelback Road. Thousands upon thousands of people drive over the underpass every day, and the vast majority of them remain completely unaware of the splendor below.

The floor of the underpass was perfect for a carpet and the perfect canvas for artists Rosario Marquardt and Roberto Behar of R&R Studios. The terrazzo *Magic Carpet* is bathed in 13 colors of Sonoran Desert flowers and the Arizona sky. Making it even more magical are the 166 butterflies woven throughout. The work was completed in May of 2007, and this award-winning project has delighted pedestrians and art lovers to this day.

The chrysalis of public beautification projects began many years ago. Following acrimonious congressional debate in Washington, DC, President Lyndon B. Johnson (1908–1973) signed the Highway Beautification Act of 1965, which reinvigorated the country's "Keep America Beautiful" program. Since the mid 1980s and early '90s, Phoenicians have realized that as it grew, many of its highways would pass through neighborhoods and practically in residents' front and back yards, which led to voter-approved funds to make our highways more visually pleasant. Early designs, and still some today, were fashioned after Native American symbols and art. Today, they're sophisticated, elaborate, and often clever.

Phoenix has a remarkable sense of responsibility and steadfast commitment to the beautification of its urban areas. Efforts stretch from pedestrian and highway bridges to exit- and on-ramps, sound barrier walls on interstates, and even the walls that mask street-facing power stations. The uncommon attention to the aesthetics of driving and walking experiences here is quite remarkable and encourages one's sense of wanderlust.

Address 2502 E Camelback Road, Phoenix, AZ 85016, www.phoenix.gov/arts/public-art-program/explore-the-collection/magic-carpet | **Getting there** Bus 50, 60, 70 to Camelback Road & 24th Street | **Hours** Unrestricted | **Tip** While you're here, spoil yourself with some upscale shopping and delicious dining at Biltmore Fashion Park (2502 E Camelback Road, www.shopbiltmore.com).

62 Majestic Tempe 7
Movie parties, curated film, and tea time

In addition to first-run, soon-to-be blockbuster hits, Majestic Tempe 7 offers exciting, engaging, and totally fun movie parties, a monthly themed curated film series, and lovely tea time-themed movie events. Part of the locally owned Majestic Neighborhood Cinema Grill family of movie houses, it also features service-at-your-seat dining that's not intrusive, including a menu of adult-only beverages. As if that wasn't enough, there's a full bar adjacent to the theatre's ticketing lobby to enjoy before or after your movie event.

Their Movie Parties are a spectacle that you have to experience. The theatre engages movie party hosts, typically a roster of 13 or 14 hosts who are passionate about the particular featured film or the theatre's movie-party programming. Different from the traditional shadow-acting of a Rocky Horror Picture Show screening (which they also offer), the Movie Parties include a host(s) introduction, usually with some trivia and/or giveaways, and participation props to enjoy throughout the film. They also offer a curated film series, a different theme every month, that features menu items matching that month's theme. Fun, right?

The overall menu is chef-driven, creative, and brilliantly takes into consideration that diners are eating in the dark. You can also enjoy coffee roasted right here in Tempe by Cartel Roasters, and a seasonal rotation of local beers.

A fan of the horror genre? You will want to check out their "Cinematcry" movies on Tuesdays. Want something a little "classier"? During the cooler months of the year, the theatre's other two locations, one in Chandler and one in Gilbert, offer Tea Time events that feature three courses of tea and treats to enjoy with a movie that's perfect for…tea time. Perhaps the best aspect of this cinematic experience is their good movie manners policies of "No Talking. No Texting. No Arriving Late."

Address 1140 E Baseline Road, Tempe, AZ 85283, +1 (480) 908-3059, www.majesticphx.com/movie-theater/majestictempe7 | Getting there Bus 77 to Baseline Road & Lakeshore Drive | Hours See website for movie and movie event times | Tip The only 70mm IMAX screen in Arizona is located at the family-owned Harkins Theatres Arizona Mills 18 (5000 South Arizona Mills Circle, Tempe, www.harkins.com/theatres/arizona-mills-18-w-imax).

63 Maricopa County Justice Museum

Where the Miranda Warning was established

"You have the right to remain silent. Anything you say can and will be used against you in a court of law. You have the right to an attorney…" The Miranda Warning is something that everyone should have heard over the last nearly sixty years. It's ubiquitous in any law enforcement television program, murder mystery movies, and the evening news. Police officers or law enforcement officials are required by law to speak these words, which are the actual rights that American citizens have when arrested as a suspect.

The Maricopa County Justice Museum & Learning Center is believed to be the only museum of its kind in an active courthouse in the United States. Maricopa County's historic Old Courthouse was restored to its 1929 grandeur in recent years and houses the Justice Museum, which chronicle's the county's legal history, its court cases – including the 1966 Miranda vs. Arizona case and its ruling – and the overall rule of law.

The main attraction is a restored cellblock on the 6th floor, the very one where the warning's namesake Ernesto Miranda (1941–1976) was housed during his 1963 arrest, the process of which would lead to the landmark US Supreme Court decision in 1966. Miranda was later paroled, but he was stabbed to death in 1976 during an argument during a card game at a downtown Phoenix bar. Notice the original, preserved prisoner artwork here.

The exhibits in the museum focus on watershed moments in Arizona's legal history, as well as exhibits that offer insights into the lives of important people in the state's legal history, including US Supreme Court Justice Sandra Day O'Connor and the Honorable Lorna Lockwood, who was the first female justice of the Arizona Supreme Court and the first female justice of any state supreme court in the nation.

Address 125 W Washington Street, Phoenix, AZ 85003, +1 (602) 506-1497, www.justicemuseum.org, tours.justicemuseumphx@gmail.com | Getting there Valley Metro Light Rail to Jefferson/1st Avenue | Hours Mon–Fri 8am–5pm | Tip The Phoenix Police Museum offers a comprehensive history and modern context of the Phoenix Police Department through interactive exhibits and historic vehicles. Its entrance is on the south side of the same building, and it's free (17 S 2nd Street, www.phoenixpolicemuseum.org).

64 Martin Auto Museum
The rise, fall, and rise again of the iconic Tucker

There were only 51 Tucker 48 cars ever built, including the one prototype. Today, the vast majority still exist primarily in museums and private collections, and the vast majority of those continue to be roadworthy. Billed as the "Car of Tomorrow" in 1948, the Tucker 48 is not only slick, but it also has innovative safety features, including seatbelts, a pop-out windshield, and a center headlight that turns with the steering wheel.

There have been only a few of them up for sale in recent years. One was purchased by a local collector at auction in January 2024 for $1.7 million dollars. The winning bid was placed by Mel Martin, the founder and chairman of the Martin Auto Museum in Glendale, just minutes from downtown Phoenix. The Tucker 48 is now on display here. What makes this particular vehicle even more unique? It was one of only four ever produced in black, making it the rarest color.

While you're visiting this mind-blowing collection, you will see an iconic 1981 DMC DeLorean of *Back to the Future* fame; a 1933 Buick Series 90 Limousine previously owned by Queen Wilhelmina of the Netherlands; the 1990 Ford NASCAR Baby Ruth Car driven by Jeff Gordon; and a 2010 Chevrolet Camaro Transformer Edition, coupled with a life-sized sculpture of Bumblebee. You can actually sit inside about 100 of the vehicles. You'll also find car models, neon signs, a carousel for the kids, and a game room for kids of all ages.

Which is Martin's favorite car? It's the one that inspired the museum's logo: a 1930 Cadillac LaSalle 340 Touring Car. He drove this car two of the four times he competed in The Great American Race. You will also see a 1966 Ford Mustang Convertible, a 1914 Ford Model T Racer, a 2015 BMW i8, 2001 Ferrari Spider, and a 1967 Chevrolet Corvette Stingray. It's impossible to list every highlight in this phenomenal collection. You have to see it all for yourself.

Address 4320 W Thunderbird Road, Glendale, AZ 85306, +1 (602) 298-2377, www.martinautomuseum.org | Getting there Bus 43, 138 to 43rd Avenue & Thunderbird Road | Hours Tue–Sun 9am–5pm | Tip The architecturally beautiful State 48 Brewery in downtown Phoenix was originally an open-air market in 1927 and later an automotive repair shop. In 2018, State 48 became the first tenant in 40 years (345 W Van Buren Street, www.state48brewery.com).

65 Mel's Diner
"Kiss my grits!"

One of the top 10 television shows in America from 1976 to 1985 was set right here in Phoenix. *Alice* was set in a diner just on the outskirts of Phoenix. In real life, the diner is mere minutes from the heart of downtown.

On the show, Mel's often served horrible food, but the food at today's Mel's Diner is your classic diner fare served by lovely servers, as likable as those from the popular series, although their hair probably isn't as big.

If you're familiar with the show, you will know you're in the right place as soon as you see the iconic "Mel's Diner" sign with the big coffee cup, often shown on the later seasons. A producer scouting Phoenix for a shot for the opening credits saw what had been Chris' Diner. That producer convinced the owner to change the name to "Mel's" for the show, and the name stuck. Adorning the walls of the diner, which is far roomier than it appeared on TV, are photographs of the cast on set, in marketing photos, and on the cover of *TV Guide*, as well as other memorabilia offering nods to the diner's role in television history.

Belly up to the counter or relax in a comfy booth. The menu features many diner classics, from omelets to club sandwiches, and many other expected dishes, but you'll also find a Greek influence. There are feta and gyro omelets, and you can even get a side of tzatziki. There's a South-of-the-Border influence too. Try the chorizo and eggs or the breakfast burrito. The diner serves only breakfast and lunch.

While not prominently featured on today's menu, can you guess the Southern staple that is mentioned in many, many episodes in the series? Alabama-born Polly Holiday, who won two Golden Globe awards while on the show, played the sassy, brash, giant-red-wig-wearing character Florence Jean "Flo" Castleberry. When provoked or irritated, Flo would gift the sitcom-loving audience an enthusiastic "Kiss my grits!"

Address 1747 Grand Avenue, Phoenix, AZ 85007, +1 (602) 252-8283 | **Getting there** Bus 17 to McDowell Road & 18th Avenue, or bus 19 to 19th Avenue & Culver Street | **Hours** Sun–Thu 7am–2pm, Fri & Sat 6am–2pm | **Tip** Enjoy stacks of the acclaimed "Best Pancakes in Phoenix" at Joe's Diner, open for breakfast and lunch. Say hello to owners Joe and Joan, who are almost always there (4515 N 7th Avenue, www.joesdineraz.com).

66 Melinda's Alley Speakeasy

Kindhearted lady of the evening

"Good deeds outweigh the sins of Malinda," was a headline in a Saturday, October 29, 1910, article in *The Arizona Republican* newspaper announcing the passing of Malinda Curtis the day before. Curtis was well known in the downtown Phoenix community for being rambunctious and kindhearted. She would help the sick and indigent and expect nothing in return. She also had a temper, but usually only when provoked, according to newspapers of the day. She was even stabbed once, which sent her to the hospital and her assailant to jail.

There has been a hotel at the corner of Central Avenue and Adams Street since 1896. The first was the Adams Hotel, not named for the street, which was named for President Adams, but for the proprietor, J. C. Adams, an attorney who moved to Phoenix from Chicago. Of the three different hotels on this spot, the Adams Hotel was welcoming guests when Curtis lived in the area. Records do not indicate when exactly she moved here, but it's believed that she was in Phoenix for at least 20 years. So she would have seen the Adams Hotel being built. In 2016, the current Renaissance Phoenix Downtown Hotel, the third hotel on this corner, opened a speakeasy named Melinda's Alley (spelled with an e rather than an a), a nod to Curtis' spirit.

On the north wall of the hotel is a 70-foot-high by 50-foot-wide, colorful mural of Malinda, with the hotel ablaze below her because it burned in 1910. Melinda's Alley speakeasy pays homage to the beloved local woman. There are no actual photographs of Malinda Curtis, so the local artists Hugo Medina and Darrin Armijo-Wardle used photos of other Black women from the era to develop this beautiful rendering. A nod to her days as a "courtesan" in Arizona mining towns, there's a red light above the door to the speakeasy, which is part of the mural. When the light is on, the speakeasy is open.

Address 50 E Adams Street, Phoenix, AZ 85004, +1 (602) 333-0000, www.visitphoenix.com/listing/melindas-alley/17572 | Getting there Light Rail to Washington/Central Avenue; bus 542, 563, or I-10 to Van Buren/Central Avenue | Hours Fri & Sat 9pm–1am | Tip Enjoy an elevated cocktail experience at Bitter & Twisted Cocktail Parlour in the historic Luhrs Building, which formerly served as the Arizona Prohibition Headquarters (1 W Jefferson Street, www.bitterandtwistedaz.com).

67 — Merci Train

49 boxcars of gratitude from France

The Gratitude Train arrived in New York Harbor on February 2, 1949 aboard the French freighter *Magellan*, to wondrous fanfare. The train was a gift of 49 boxcars filled with one million gifts from the citizens of France, a *"Merci"* for the previous gift from the US of 700 rail cars filled with food, fuel, and clothing for France and Italy after World War II. There was an individual boxcar for each state at the time, and one for Washington, DC and Hawaii to share.

The olive-green boxcars, made of oak with iron framework, are adorned with the colorful coat of arms of the 40 provinces of France and a wooden, horizontal, blue, white, and red sash across the side of each car. One side reads, "Gratitude Train," and the other side reads, *"Train de La Reconnaissance Française."* Also on each side is the Great Seal of the United States, and another marking in French, "*40 hommes, 8 chevaux*," fully understood by the Doughboys of World War I to mean that the capacity of each car is 40 men or 8 horses.

Among the generous, heartfelt gifts from the citizens of France were bicycles, paintings, dolls, books, clothing, medals, a wedding dress, and so much more. The gifts were not meant for individuals but as "the permanent property of the people" for use in schools, museums, and other institutions. Today, many of those gifts are on display at the Arizona State Capitol Museum, which offers free admission.

The Arizona boxcar was moved to McCormick-Stillman Railroad Park in the late 1980s following a restoration effort by Zina Kuhn, the one-woman force behind the restoration of Arizona's Merci Train. Grateful to the United States for granting her citizenship when she came from Soviet Russia following World War II, she cited a quote from President Kennedy as the motivation for the years-long effort, "Ask not what your country can do for you, but what you can do for your country."

Address 7301 E Indian Bend Road, Scottsdale, AZ 85250, +1 (480) 312-2312, www.therailroadpark.com, therailroadpark@scottsdaleaz.gov | Getting there Bus 72 to Scottsdale & Indian Bend Roads | Hours See website for seasonal hours | Tip In nearby Camelback Cemetery, the first to serve Greater Scottsdale, is a monument dedicated to the American Legion, "In memory to those who served…" (6820 E McDonald Drive, Paradise Valley).

68 Mexican Arts Imports

A mecca for Mexican arts

Ashley Diaz, one of four generations of her family to live in Arizona, remembers when the historic building that houses Mexican Arts Imports was painted white. While her grandfather Fred Montez Sr. was traveling, Diaz's father painted the building bright yellow. Grandfather was not happy about it, but from a marketing and directional perspective, it was a brilliant move. You can't miss the yellow building that was once a salsa factory, a staple food that traces back to Aztecs, Incas, and Mayans.

When you walk in the front door, you see the bright colors of the many art objects, as well as the bright and welcoming faces of the people who work here – Southwestern hospitality at its finest. Go right, left, or straight ahead, as a labyrinth of magnificent Mexican arts unfolds before your very eyes. Throughout the thousands of square feet of shopping space, you will find a variety of art, with concentrations of specific styles in certain areas. To the right, you'll find an abundance of *santos*, art objects of veneration in Latino cultural tradition and religious life. To the left, you will find *huipiles*, scarves, and denim, as well as intricately designed leather holsters and beautiful tin and tile mirrors.

The most sought-after items in the shop? Diaz says it's definitely anything cactus, especially the saguaro cactus, as it is synonymous with the Southwest. Another top seller is their talavera ceramics, the brightly colored Day of the Dead sculptures, pots, bowls, vases, and chihuahuas – the list goes on and on, and this art form's popularity seems eternal.

Be sure to venture outside, where you will discover yet another world, this one with large pots and statuary, as well as metal extraterrestrials, colorful cacti, and life-sized, rearing Azteca horses. The company started in 1968. For good reason, Diaz excitedly predicts, "The first 50-plus years are just the beginning."

Address 340 N 24th Street, Phoenix, AZ 85008, +1 (602) 275-9552 | Getting there
Bus 3, 70 to Van Buren & 24th Streets | Hours Mon–Fri 9am–5pm, Sat 9:30am–3:30pm,
Sun 10am–2pm | Tip Enjoy the live Mariachi Brunch at Tequila Cocina & Cantina,
featuring modern Mexican cuisine inspired by Jalisco. They serve lunch and dinner daily,
too (4818 N 7th Street, www.tequilaphx.com).

69 The Onion House

Evans House, among the oldest private homes

No, this isn't a market, a restaurant, or even a museum. It's called The Onion House for its rather unique shape, at least unique in Phoenix, specifically its onion dome over the semi-circular front porch. The Evans House is one of the oldest surviving Queen Anne-Victorian homes in the city, one of only three remaining. Built in 1893 for $6,000, a whopping cost at the time, the home had six bedrooms and palatial, 12-foot-high pocket doors opening to a room with 15-foot-high ceilings. It was the home of Dr. John M. and Jennie Evans. This well-known couple lived in the downstairs of the house and Dr. Evans used the upstairs as his office, accessible by an exterior staircase.

In 1908, the husband-and-wife physician team of Oscar and Virginia Mahoney bought the home, which would be their residence until 1924 when Virginia passed away. The Evans House became a boarding home, and it was placed on the National Register of Historic Places in 1978, a move that surely helped ensure its survival. At that time, it was one of only three of an original eleven buildings noted in a 1940 survey of historical structures that had not yet been torn down.

The State of Arizona purchased the house in 1981. During a 1987–1988 restoration, the exterior staircase was enclosed to add two restrooms, as most Queen Anne residences of the era only had one indoor bathroom. The restoration cost half a million dollars. Great care was taken to ensure the authenticity of the style. No Phillips screws were used because they had not yet been invented when the house was constructed.

Immediately across the street is the 1907 Carnegie Public Library, a much larger structure. The Onion House is nestled between a six-story building and a relatively tall parking structure, making it easy to miss this historic beauty, so keep your eyes open as you can freely walk its entire perimeter.

Address 1100 W Washington Street, Phoenix, AZ 85007 | **Getting there** Bus DASH, GAL, I-10, I-17, SME, SMW, SR 51 to Washington Street & 12th Avenue | **Hours** Unrestricted | **Tip** The J. W. Walker / Central Arizona Light & Power Building was built in 1920 by Phoenix businessman and real estate developer J. W. Walker. A Stickler's Café today, it retains a great amount of its historical architectural detail (30 N 3rd Avenue, www.sticklersaz.com).

70 Origin of Phoenix Newspapers

A plaque marks the city's first newspapers

On E Van Buren Street, just west of 2nd Street, is a plaque that commemorates the first newspapers in Phoenix. The inscription begins, "The ARIZONA REPUBLIC is directly descended from the Valley's first newspaper, The SALT RIVER HERALD, first published January 26, 1878."

The city's very first newspaper was launched only a few years after the Phoenix townsite had officially been incorporated in 1881 and decades before Arizona was granted statehood in 1912. The brown placard with silver border and lettering was installed by the Phoenix Historical Society and the Arizona Historical Society. It is placed at a large traffic intersection, and you can easily miss it, which is a shame, given the site's significant history in the telling of this important piece of the history of Phoenix.

Not surprisingly, some of the earliest leaders of Phoenix newspapers were leaders of the Arizona Territory from February 24, 1863 until February 14, 1912, when it became the State of Arizona. One notable owner of the *Arizona Republican* (today the *Arizona Republic*) was Dwight Bancroft Heard. He purchased the paper in 1912 and published it until his death in 1929. A few months later, his namesake Heard Museum opened. In 1946, Eugene C. Pulliam of Indianapolis bought *The Phoenix Gazette* (ceased in 1997) and *The Arizona Republic* newspapers for $4 million. He would form Phoenix Newspapers Inc. and ran both Arizona newspapers and others until he died in 1975. Throughout its history *The Arizona Republic* endorsed political candidates and often met with backlash and highly vocal public opinion. It ceased doing so in 2020.

Across the street is today's *Arizona Republic* headquarters, with "The Arizona Republic" lettered across the top of the building.

Address E Van Buren & 2nd Streets, www.hmdb.org/m.asp?m=126695 | Getting there
Bus 514, 521, 522, 532, 533, 535, 542 to Van Buren & 1st Streets | Hours Unrestricted | Tip
American Family Fields of Phoenix, the Spring Training home of the Milwaukee Brewers,
is one of ten stadiums across the Valley of the Sun to host ballgames in February and March
each year (3805 N 53rd Avenue, www.mlb.com/brewers/spring-training/ballpark).

71 Palm Lane

A Hollywood-like drive without the LA traffic

Looking west down W Palm Lane between 7th and 11th Avenues, you will see the iconic Arizona Veterans Memorial Coliseum on the horizon. This spot is an oasis reminiscent of the classic Hollywood movies with characters driving in convertibles down palm-lined streets in Los Angeles. Palm Lane, although non-contiguous and not in a straight line, stretches east-to-west more than 50 miles across Metro Phoenix. It has numerous blocks that are beautifully lined with palm trees, which were planted as part of the neighborhood development plan in 1930.

The Coliseum, still active today, has enjoyed many notable visitors, including several US presidents, who have visited Arizona since before it was granted statehood. In 1901, President William McKinley (1843–1901) noted in a public speech, "The country has become so large…that it takes at least 40 days to reach the outlying possessions of this republic."

Today, that same trip takes less than five hours by plane, and several presidents have come to the Arizona Veterans Memorial Coliseum since its opening in 1965. Perhaps more exciting, the Coliseum has also served as a venue for Phoenix teams representing the professional sports of basketball, hockey, tennis, indoor soccer, and roller derby. Musically, it has hosted talented giants, including Elvis, Prince, and Snoop Dogg. It's also the centerpiece at the annual Arizona State Fair.

You can find this scenic photo op situated in the Encanto Palmcroft Historic District, developed between 1925 and 1949. The proximity of the neighborhood to parks represents an approach to suburban planning that had its roots in 18th-century England. "Croft" is an English word meaning "garden," and palm is self-explanatory, hence Palmcroft, one of the most beautiful and elegant neighborhoods in all of Phoenix. There are only 330 homes in the neighborhood, and it boasts 222 acres of park land.

Address W Palm Lane between N 7th & N 11th Avenues, Phoenix, AZ 85007, www.encantopalmcroft.org | **Getting there** Bus 15 to 15th Avenue & Palm Lane, or bus 8 to 7th Avenue & Palm Lane | **Hours** Unrestricted | **Tip** Popular for generations, the most photographed place on Arizona State University's campus is their spectacular Palm Walk (ASU Campus, Tempe, https://tours.asu.edu/tempe/palm-walk).

72 Papago Park Amphitheater

3,500-seats now abandoned

Nestled between deep red buttes on nearly every side, the Papago Park Amphitheater has been long abandoned. But it was once a lively place to enjoy some entertainment in a beautiful setting. You can easily imagine the thrill of just coming here. To the northwest is Barnes Butte, and east of that is an often clear view of the horizon, where you may see snow-capped mountains to the northeast, just beyond the Papago Sports Complex.

Walk up the center aisle of the amphitheater and continue to the summit between the two buttes immediately behind the amphitheater, and you'll discover a majestic view of Tempe, one of Phoenix's neighboring cities and part of Metro Phoenix. That city has changed more in the last few decades than these buttes have in millions of years. South from this vista are the Desert Botanical Garden, the Hole in the Rock, the Phoenix Zoo, and the Hall of Flame Museum, as well as the Salt River, which runs immediately north of Tempe. Should you climb west of the amphitheater, you will enjoy vistas of downtown Phoenix, particularly beautiful at sunset.

Since the early 1930s and for many decades, Papago Park Amphitheater was most famous for the popular Easter sunrise services held here. If you are new to Phoenix, you will be delighted at the spectacle of sunrises that rival the most beautiful sunsets in many other places. They are truly spectacular and attracted thousands to those sunrise services. The amphitheater was also host to high school and civic organization concerts, college picnics, a meeting of 3,000 Missourians interested in vacationing in Metro Phoenix, and speeches by the Arizona governor. Originally constructed in 1933 by the Civilian Conservation Corps, the amphitheater has been mostly abandoned for 50 years. Today it only attracts the occasional hiker. It did, however, see a partial restoration in 2010, an Eagle Scout project.

Address McDowell Road between E Karsten Way & N Galvin Parkway, Phoenix, AZ 85008 | Getting there Bus 17 to McDowell Road & Karsten Way | Hours Daily dawn–dusk | Tip Opened in 1964, the historic Celebrity Theatre has hosted Etta James, Duran Duran, Diana Ross, Grateful Dead, Beyoncé, David Bowie, and Lynyrd Skynyrd. An in-the-round theater, no seat is more than 70 feet from the stage (440 N 32nd Street, www.celebritytheatre.com).

73 Peacock Staircase

Mae West and others graced these stairs

The ornate, Spanish Baroque-style Orpheum Theatre opened in 1929, months before the Great Depression, and thrilled audiences with talking movies and Vaudeville acts. The Corona family leased the theater in the 1970s and early 1980s, showing movies and hosting events primarily for the local Hispanic community. But the theater's star faded as Phoenix expanded.

Fortunately, it was saved by historic preservation efforts and re-opened in 1997 with a performance of *Hello, Dolly!* starring Carol Channing (1921–2019). After the show, Channing thanked the Phoenicians for not turning this crown jewel into a parking lot.

One of the theater's most beautiful features is its magnificent peacock staircase at the south end of the lobby. Look up to see the majestic birds gracing the underside of the elliptical stairway, which recently inspired the Orpheum's new logo. Revealed in June of 2024, the logo features a peacock within a color palette inspired by "blending interior features and contemporary desert tones," according to the theater's website.

The historic theatre has welcomed many celebrities. If these walls could talk, they would spew forth encyclopedic volumes of stories of Hollywood fame, cinematic favorites, and some one-liners that will be remembered for eons. The original blonde bombshell Mae West visited the Orpheum at least twice, once in 1933 to promote her film *I'm No Angel,* and again in 1951 as the star in her stage play *Diamond Lil.*

The Orpheum is today owned and operated by the City of Phoenix, the stewards of preserving this iconic Phoenix treasure and scheduling programming for today and the future. You can go on a free tour of the theater, including haunted history tours in the fall. Performances in recent decades have included *Ancient Aliens* to Celtic Women, Chaka Khan to Rodrigo Y Gabriela, Susan Boyle to William Shatner, and Margaret Cho to Matteo Lane.

Address 203 W Adams Street, Phoenix, AZ 85003, +1 (602) 262-7272, www.fototphx.org |
Getting there Valley Metro Light Rail to Jefferson / 1st Avenue; bus 542, 563, 575, GAL,
I-10, I-17, SMW, SR 51 to Adams Street & 3rd Avenue | Hours See website for event and
tour schedule | Tip The Wildlife World Zoo, opened in 1984, was built from the ground
up by a local resident and hosts more than 600 individual exotic and endangered species
(16501 W Northern Avenue, Litchfield Park, www.wildlifeworld.com).

74 Penske Racing Museum

Cars, trophies, and racing legends

If speed gives you a thrill, you will find the Penske Racing Museum incredibly exciting. Your adrenaline increases exponentially as you enter this two-story gallery of racing winners and automobiles of prestigious stature. You'll want to speed through to see everything, but do make yourself slow down enough to absorb the significant history you are experiencing. You are walking among legends of the racing world, including a replica of the 1963 Pontiac Catalina that Roger Penske, founder of Penske Corporation, drove to victory in the 1963 NASCAR Riverside 250.

This modest yet magnificent and diverse collection of racing cars includes several cars that won the Indianapolis 500, some NAS-CAR racers, and Pace Cars, traditionally given to the winner of the Indy 500. The 1972 Hurst Olds on display was the tribute to Mark Donohue's (1937–1975) victory in 1972, the first in a long line of Team Penske wins in more than 600 major races. Some of the cars you will see were made by Ford, Dodge, Chevrolet, Pontiac, and Porsche. And displayed throughout are gigantic trophies on pedestals. Take a good look at the car engines here too, which are elevated on posts with placards detailing the technical specs – a goldmine of information for any motorhead. The placards show specific race win(s) and the drivers of those wins.

Then there's the pathway to the test track in the back of the property. The path itself is paved with bricks stamped "W.C. CO., CULVER BLOCK, PAT. MAY 21, 1901," showcasing the rich history of Indianapolis Motor Speedway. These bricks are the originals. Finally, the museum has a café on the second floor, where you can enjoy breakfast or lunch amidst Penske's collection of trophies and models, or on the mezzanine overlooking the test track, while daydreaming about driving one of these splendid pieces of racing history across the finish line.

Address 7191 E Chauncey Lane, Phoenix, AZ 85054, +1 (480) 538-4444,
www.penskeautomall.com/penske-racing-museum | **Getting there** Bus 72 to Scottsdale
Road & Chauncey Lane | **Hours** Mon–Sat 10am–4pm, Sun noon–5pm | **Tip** Octane
Raceway is the only full-time indoor/outdoor kart racing track in the entire United States.
They also offer axe-throwing and a free-roam, multiplayer, virtual-reality experience.
(9119 E Talking Stick Way, Scottsdale, www.octaneraceway.com).

75 Petroglyph Preserve
Art, cultural, way-making, or religious icons?

You have probably seen petroglyphs on television, in a textbook, or maybe in a museum. But at the Deer Valley Petroglyph Preserve, managed by Arizona State University, you get to see these ancient works where they were made. Petroglyphs date back to around 8,000 B.C. – the ones you will see here at Hedgpeth Hills date back to approximately 3,000 B.C.E. through 500 C.E. and are attributed to three different Native American cultures: Western Archaic, Hohokam, and Patayan. The vast majority of the 1,500 cataloged petroglyphs here were likely created by the Hohokam, the same culture that created the canals in the area that led to the settlement of what is today Metro Phoenix.

Despite the scarcity of water in the Sonoran Desert, it has one of the most diverse ecosystems on the planet, some of which you will get to experience as you explore the petroglyphs. The quarter-mile path features educational placards, as well as warnings to stay on the trail because you're in a rattlesnake habitat. You will see several instances of creosote, a toxic desert shrub that was used by Native Americans as an antibacterial treatment for open wounds, colds, fevers, ulcers, and liver and kidney issues. Today, it's being scientifically studied as a potential use in cancer treatment.

As you make your way along this linear gravel walking trail, you will find the largest concentration of petroglyphs at the end. Pause here. The more time you give your eyes to adjust to the light, the more you will see. There are also viewing tubes through which you will see a few highlighted specimens. The petroglyphs have been studied for ages, and the preserve opened in December 1994. While you can learn a lot about the geography, flora, fauna, the massive hill behind the building, and the history of the surrounding area, the meaning of the petroglyph shapes and symbols pecked into these ancient rocks remains a mystery.

Address 3711 W Deer Valley Road, Glendale, AZ 85308, +1 (623) 582-8007, https://deervalley.asu.edu, dvpp@asu.edu | Getting there Bus 35 to 35th Avenue & Deer Valley Road | Hours See website for seasonal hours | Tip Adobe Dam Regional Park is home to Six Flags Hurricane Harbor, Go-Kart Racing, Maricopa Live Steamers, the Arizona Model Pilots Society, and more (23280 N 43rd Avenue, Glendale, www.maricopacountyparks.net/park-locator/adobe-dam-regional-park).

76 PHX Cat Café
Helping kitties find their 'fur-ever' homes

Located on the north side of downtown, the PHX Cat Café is considerably more than a pet placement service. It's a comfortable space to spend time among cats and maybe even adopt one. The non-profit venue partnered with Kate Benjamin, a nationally celebrated cat behavior expert and author of the blog *Modern Cat*, who helped with the "catification" of the space. Resident kitties enjoy wall-mounted lounger shelves and cubbies. There are sofas, chairs, benches, and tables for humans and cats alike. You are invited to enjoy a beverage from the full-service coffee shop, which offers locally roasted coffee by Passport Coffee, as well as tea, smoothies, Italian sodas, and a few snacks.

CEO Carrie Schwartz, who has a master's degree in animal behavior, can usually tell when someone is a perfect match with one of the feline residents. She always keeps human and cat harmony and happiness front of mind, but you don't have to have a plan to adopt to spend time with your new furry friends, as walk-ins are welcome. But for the cats' safety and wellbeing, the number of visitors is limited, so reservations are strongly encouraged.

For the comfort of the cats and out of respect for other visitors, everyone is asked to please obey "The Catmandments," a list of rules posted in the lounge, which are mostly common sense. The café also offers fun cat-themed merchandise, including coffee mugs, t-shirts, water bottles, and totes. And check out the adorable stickers. When a feline resident has lived in the PHX Cat Café for a year, a custom sticker is made in its honor. That cat's face is incorporated into the café's logo, which features a cat sitting in a coffee cup. It's purr-fect!

PHX Cat Café hosts a number of special events, too, including Yoga with Cats, Kitten Yoga, Drag Bingo, and Paint Nights. Get your tickets online. These popular events do sell out!

Address 147 E Garfield Street, Phoenix, AZ 85004, www.phxcatcafe.org, info@phxcatcafe.org | Getting there Valley Metro Light Rail to Roosevelt / Central Avenue; bus 0, 10 to Central Avenue & McKinley Street | Hours Thu 10am–2pm & 3–6pm, Fri & Sat 10am–2pm & 3–8pm, Sun 10am–2pm & 3–6pm | Tip Land animals are great fun, as are sea creatures! Visit SEA LIFE Arizona to see sharks, seahorses, stingrays, and always festive clownfish (5000 S Arizona Mills Circle, Tempe, www.visitsealife.com/arizona).

77 — Piestewa Peak

The first Native American woman killed in combat

Piestewa Peak was named for Lori Ann Piestewa (1979–2003), a member of the Hopi Tribe and the first Native American woman to die in combat while serving in the US military. She was also the first woman in the US military killed in the Iraq War.

According to the National Museum of the United States Army, Piestewa was the third generation of her family to join the military, following in the footsteps of her grandfather and father. She volunteered with the 507th Maintenance Company in 2003 and was deployed to Iraq in February. In March, her convoy was ambushed in Nasiriyah, Iraq. She and several other soldiers were captured, and she died of injuries sustained during the ambush while a prisoner of war. She was 23 years old.

The State of Arizona renamed what was once known as Squaw Peak in Piestewa's honor in 2003, mere weeks after her death. Also renamed in 2003 was State Route 51, formerly Squaw Peak Parkway. Today, it's the Piestewa Freeway.

Piestewa was awarded the Purple Heart and the Prisoner of War Medal, and she was posthumously promoted from private first class to specialist. The renamings bring to light that regardless of our different backgrounds, we all come together to defend our nation.

The placards showing the dedication to Piestewa are located in the ramada at the south end of the Mesquite Trailhead, the second parking area going into the Phoenix Mountains Preserve, which is the first one on the left. This trailhead is long, so if you park or enter at the north end, head south back toward Phoenix to find the two markers. You can start your climb to the summit here, too.

Some hikers compare Piestewa Peak to hiking Camelback Mountain. While it is a challenging hike, it's a bit less difficult than Camelback. There are rails for some of the more treacherous elevations. Remember to be just as careful coming back down.

Address 2701 Piestewa Peak Drive, Phoenix, AZ 85016, + 1 (602) 261-8318, www.phoenix.gov/parks/trails/locations/piestewa-peak | **Getting there** By car, take SR 51 to Exit 5, then turn east onto E Glendale Avenue and turn left onto Piestewa Peak Drive | **Hours** See website for seasonal hours | **Tip** At the southern foothills of Piestewa Peak is the Frank Lloyd Wright-inspired Arizona Biltmore where the Tequila Sunrise cocktail was invented in the 1930s (2400 E Missouri Avenue, www.arizonabiltmore.com).

78 Pioneer Memorial Park

Seven historic cemeteries dating 1884 to 1914

Practically steps from the Arizona State Capitol is a cemetery that is the final resting place of politicians, cowboys, farmers, military figures, and prostitutes, as well as many of Phoenix's prestigious (and otherwise) founders. Pioneer & Military Memorial Park (PMMP) is not the prettiest graveyard you'll ever see, but it holds the graves of many early Phoenix celebrities. There are efforts underway to make certain gravesites and the whole park a more inviting place overall and to give it the reverence it deserves, especially given all that its residents contributed to Phoenix. There are thousands of stories here in the city's oldest cemetery.

PMMP comprises seven historic cemeteries that were in use between 1884 and its closing in 1914. They are: Ancient Order of United Workmen (AOUW), Independent Order of Odd Fellows (IOOF), Knights of Pythias (KofP), City/Loosley, Masons, Porter, and Rosedale.

Look for the grave of Jacob Waltz (1808–1891), section XIX in City/Loosley Cemetery. He was better known as The Lost Dutchman. He was actually a native of Germany. If you have lived in Metro Phoenix for any period of time, you have likely heard the story of "The Lost Dutchman's Mine." As the story goes, he and his partner Jacob Weiser worked in a fabled gold mine in the Superstition Mountains. After Weiser's death, Waltz supposedly hid a significant stash of gold. Twenty years later, he told his caretaker where it was, but no one has yet found it.

Phillip Darrell Duppa (1832–1892), buried in Mason's Cemetery, was one of the founders of Phoenix and is credited with naming the new townsite, as well as Tempe. His 1870 home (115 W Sherman Street) is the oldest standing home in Phoenix. Judge John T. Alsap (1830–1886) was a politician, physician, and farmer. He was the first Treasurer of Arizona Territory and the first Mayor of Phoenix in 1881.

Address 1317 W Jefferson Street, Phoenix, AZ 85007, https://www.azhistcemeteries.org/our-cemeteries.html, pioneercem@yahoo.com | Getting there Bus 514, 521, 522, 532, 533, 535, 542, 562 to Jefferson Avenue & 15th Street | Hours Thu 10am–2pm by appointment, viewing unrestricted from the street | Tip Recently rededicated after years of neglect, Cementerio Lindo, Spanish for "Pretty Cemetery," has more than 7,800 graves, including those of some of Phoenix's earliest settlers (1648 S 15th Avenue).

79 Pip Coffee + Clay

Make a mug that looks like your dog

One of the best reasons to take a class at Pip Coffee + Clay? Because you can. Think about all the fun activities you did as a kid that are not available to you as an adult, even when you have the spare time. Pip Coffee + Clay – Pip being short for "Perpetual Idea Project" – reinvigorates your passion for creativity and does so in a lively atmosphere. Even better, all skill levels are welcome. Wife and husband team Mara Friedman and KC Bonnem consider their fantastic space an "entertainment venue," where you get to create a one-of-a-kind keepsake. You'll often find them hosting a "motley crew" on a mission to have fun.

One of the more popular classes is Build Your Pet, where you can create your pet's furry, feathery, or scaly likeness as a bowl or mug. In the Plant Buddies class, you can make a festive planter, vase, or fruit bowl, or something akin to an olive boat. The Mugs and Hugs class is just that. You'll make a mug so adorable you'll want to give it a hug. There's also a class dedicated to making bongs in which you can enjoy your "special herbs" (legal in Arizona). The majority of the provided glazes are food, dishwasher, and microwave safe. The primary techniques offered are wheel-throwing and hand-building.

Pip's first public art installation of nearly 70 ceramic pieces was at the downtown Harumi Sushi when the sushi bar expanded in late 2023. While you're there admiring Mara's ceramic talent, try the gyoza and some real wasabi. But when you're at Pip Coffee + Clay, enjoy some locally roasted coffee, house-made and gluten-free pastries, or locally sourced burritos and bagels. They also offer beer, wine, and specialty cocktails, perfect for private parties and corporate events.

And on Mondays, Pip offers Stitch 'n' Bitch sessions, a gathering for people who enjoy making textile art in a more social atmosphere – a fun-seeking motley crew indeed.

Address 2617 N 24th Street, Phoenix, AZ 85008, +1 (480) 616-0004,
www.pipcoffeeclay.com, info@pipcoffeeclay.com | Getting there Bus 70 to 24th & Yale
Streets | Hours Mon–Fri 7:30am–9pm, Sat 8:30am–9pm, Sun 8:30am–4pm | Tip Want to
see some truly giant pots? Check out *Wall Cycle to Ocotillo*, a public art installation to beautify
highway sound barriers and walls (SR 51 bicycle trail from Brill Street to Ocotillo Road,
www.phoenix.gov/arts/public-art-program/explore-the-collection/wall-cycle-to-ocotillo).

80 _ Ponderosa Stables

Spectacular valley views, especially at sunset

Nothing represents the serenity of the American West better than the silhouette of a rider, in a cowboy hat, on a horse, at sunset. And you can have this experience yourself.

Hop in your horseless carriage and bring your friends to Ponderosa Stables, just inside South Mountain Preserve, one of the largest municipally managed parks in the United States. As you approach Ponderosa, you'll enter through a massive, iron cactus gate. The offices look like an old ghost town, with playful signage. And of course, you'll see dozens of horses.

Ponderosa Stables was founded in 1975 by Texan Rex Ross Walker. The wranglers are all volunteers (but feel free to offer them a gratuity). They're very friendly, and they'll take good care of you, with a keen focus on safety. Some of them came here to take a ride just like you before they started volunteering here.

There are various rides available, and kids are welcome, in the morning, during the day, and at sunset. One sunset option includes an hour ride across the mountain preserve, with magnificent views of the valley and up-close encounters with desert life. You'll also stop for dinner at T-Bone Steakhouse, followed by an hour's ride back under the stars. This option is perfect for celebrating a special occasion, a romantic date night, or even just because.

South Mountain Preserve boasts more than 16,000 acres and three mountain ranges: the Ma Ha Tauk, Gila, and Guadalupe. The park features more than 100 miles of trails for hiking, horseback riding, and mountain biking. One of the easiest and best ways to orient yourself is simply to look for the iconic radio towers on South Mountain. From anywhere in the Valley, you will know that you're looking south when you see those towers. While the immediate land around the towers is not open to the public, you'll have the opportunity to take photos of them on your horse ride.

Address 10215 S Central Avenue, Phoenix, AZ 85042, +1 (602) 268-1261, www.arizona-horses.com | **Getting there** By car, take S Central Avenue south to destination inside South Mountain Preserve | **Hours** Daily 7am–dusk by reservation only | **Tip** For more spectacular views of the Valley of the Sun, sunrise through sunset, check out Papago Park's Hole in the Rock, an actual hole large enough for numerous humans in a natural, geological formation (625 N Galvin Parkway, www.phoenix.gov/parks/trails/locations/papago-park).

81 _Prince Tribute Mural_

Let's go crazy for Phoenix mural culture

One day, while sitting in her hair salon, artist Maggie Keane noticed that the exterior wall on the building across the street that once hosted a colorful mandala had been painted purple. She knew that she had found the perfect location for her *Prince Tribute Mural*, a work that she'd been envisioning for years. She immediately went over and spoke with the owner of the building, which houses the Rodriguez Boxing Club, who told her that he had been approached by numerous artists who wanted to paint on that wall. But her idea resonated the most with his own vision for the purple wall, and he gave Keane the green light.

Devoted fans of Prince (1958–2016) make pilgrimages to this 47-foot-long mural on his birthday, album debut anniversaries, or for themed gatherings that include a *Purple Rain* movie night, a film for which he won a 1985 Oscar for Best Music, Original Song Score. One of the most celebrated entertainers ever, Prince composed music, wrote lyrics, played many instruments, and arranged and produced albums. Keane has captured the inimitable showmanship, looks, and milestones throughout the career of this multi-Grammy Award winner.

Prince had a history of topping *Billboard Magazine*'s charts. Keane's illustrious career has some interesting, unexpected highlights too – including once painting billboards. She was a courtroom illustrator for years and sketched the case of the 1976 murder of *Arizona Republic* investigative reporter Don Bolles (1928–1976). She helped restore and repaint the horses and rounding boards on the historic Encanto Carousel.

While working on the large, photo-realistic, central figure of Prince and his *Purple Rain* stylings, Keane had an epiphany and immediately set out to add gigantic mirrors to Prince's glasses that now reflect the world passing by. For Keane, this mural is as much of a signature piece as "When Doves Cry" was for Prince.

Address 1350 W Roosevelt Street, Phoenix, AZ 85007, www.instagram.com/maggiekeanezart | **Getting there** Bus 5 to 15th Avenue & Roosevelt Street | **Hours** Unrestricted | **Tip** Visit Keane's Black History mural as well. It features Whitney Houston, Diana Ross, and Aretha Franklin (1 E Portland Street).

82 The Psycho Building

Classic scenes from Psycho filmed in Phoenix

The opening scene of Alfred Hitchcock's most famous and most profitable thriller *Psycho* – considered the #1 horror film on some movie lists – was partially filmed in Phoenix. The pan of the city's skyline is followed by a zoom-in shot into an upper floor window of a downtown hotel. That building still stands at E Jefferson Street and S Central Avenue. The camera enters the hotel on the fifth floor of the Central Avenue side, the actual front of the building.

The building itself originally opened as a hotel and was quite the sensation. "This day promises long to remain an epoch-making occasion in the hotel circles of the Southwest. For this is the day chosen by the proprietors of the Jefferson Hotel, the newest and most modern hostelry in this section of the United States, for the formal opening," stated the *Arizona Republican* on Thursday, July 15, 1915. The Jefferson Hotel's rooftop garden warranted its own article in a special edition of the newspaper. This building was the tallest one in Arizona, New Mexico, and Nevada, and would remain the tallest in Arizona for five years.

Today, the building's future use is unsure. A plaque on the front notes its former name, the Barrister Building, and it was briefly home to the Phoenix Police Museum. Its place in Hollywood celebrity, however, is steadfast. Phoenix celebrates Psycho Day every December 11, which is the day noted in the opening sequence as the camera begins to zoom in on this landmark building.

Psycho premiered in New York City in June 1960 and debuted in Phoenix in August at the Paramount Theatre, today's Orpheum Theatre, as well as the Indian Drive-In, formerly at Indian School Road and 27th Avenue. The film site for the panning scene of the Phoenix skyline was on the southwest rooftop corner of today's Orpheum Lofts. Opened January 1931, that Art Deco building was once the tallest office building in Arizona.

Address 5 E Jefferson Street, Phoenix, AZ 85034, www.dtphx.org/2023/06/22/
the-jefferson-hotel-downtown-phoenixs-original-garden-spot | Getting there Valley Metro
Light Rail to Jefferson/1st Avenue | Hours Unrestricted from outside | Tip Also in the
opening scene of *Psycho* is the "Valley National Bank" sign, then the world's largest revolving
sign. Enjoy a Hitchcock-themed cocktail at the Floor 13 Rooftop Bar in that building,
today's Hilton Garden Inn (15 E Monroe Street, www.floor13rooftopbar.com).

83 Rainbow Wings Photo-Op

An open-armed welcome to the LGBTQIA+ community

When the new owners of Stacy's @ Melrose Christopher Tong and Brandon Slayton took the reins, they promised to keep the iconic *Rainbow Wings* mural by local artist Geremy Cites front and center as a favorite, festive, and fantastic photo-op.

The one-mile-long, historic Melrose District dates back to 1928. According to an article in *The Arizona Republic*, it was around 2006 that Melrose District began to see a resurgence. The streetscape improvements, beautification projects, and entertainment and shopping offerings have grown exponentially since then. In 2013, the same year that Stacy's opened, the Melrose District Gateway was erected at the entrance to the district. Melrose is also called "The Curve," which is depicted on the gateway structure with a pink line running through the O in Melrose, a nod to 7th Avenue's noted s-curve that's a departure from the straight-line streets on the grid.

Melrose, Phoenix's "gayborhood," is known for its eclectic vibe. It's home to many of the city's gay bars, independent cafés, coffee shops, diners, and restaurants, including some James Beard award winners and nominees. You'll find some of the best antique, vintage, and thrift shops, as well as art galleries, patio cocktailing, and dancing. Look for one of the city's two rainbow crosswalks just a few steps south of Stacy's. There is an abundance of rainbow flags along the strip, and you can get your oil changed, get a tattoo, and go to church while you're here. Eclectic is just the tip of the iceberg, and everyone is welcome!

As you approach Stacy's from the north, it's hard to miss the colossal rainbow wings mural with a white space where you can stand for your portrait. Geremy Cites is a Phoenix artist self-described as a "nerdy scientist who likes to make art." He only started creating murals in 2018. You will want to keep your eyes on this promising young artist.

Address 4343 N 7th Avenue, Phoenix, AZ 85013, +1 (480) 621-7747, www.stacysatmelrose.com, hello@stacysatmelrose.com | Getting there Bus 8 to N 7th & W Glenrosa Avenues | Hours Unrestricted | Tip Grab some friends and make your own rainbow *Abbey Road* photo just one block south (N 7th & W Glenrosa Avenues, www.phoenixpride.org/phoenix-rainbow-crosswalk).

84   Rancher Hat Bar

Design your own cowboy hat

When you were a kid, did you ever dress up like and pretend to be a cowboy? Now you get to play cowboy all over again at Rancher Hat Bar, where you can design your very own cowboy hat and take it home the same day.

Rancher Hat Bar was first on the scene to offer this unique, hands-on experience – even real cowboys of the Wild West didn't have as much say in designing their hats. But today, you can lasso your very own cowboy experience by designing a souvenir of your travels to Arizona or creating a style statement for a celebration or special event. Horse not included. Actually, you can have a horse branded onto your hat, so sometimes the horse is included.

You can go on your own (walk-ins are welcome), but this experience is great fun with a group of friends. First, you choose the style of your cowboy hat, selecting your preferred crown, crease, dent, and roll. Then you get to choose your favorite color, perhaps classic black or brown, or pink, green, or red, to name a few options. Next, head to the accessory wall to select your band and other design elements, including charms, feathers, pins, and more. There are many to choose from. Then add a brand or burnt playing cards – this is a chance to express yourself even more.

Rancher Hat Bar currently has two locations, one each in the two owners' hometowns. Shantelle Girard, from Scottsdale, AZ, and Kenny Girard, from Folsom, CA, are highly supportive of local startups and will often host events with them. They themselves first opened in January 2023 in a vintage camper trailer before opening their stores. The hats are American-made, and the branding irons are made by a local husband-and-wife team. They're also giving back to the community by partnering with charities like the Love Pup Foundation. Be among the first to enjoy this experience. Rancher Hat Bar may one day be a household name.

Address 4225 N Scottsdale Road, Scottsdale, AZ 85251, +1 (480) 334-1076, www.rancherhatbar.com, admin@rancherhatbar.com | **Getting there** By car, take I-10 east to Exit 147A, continue onto the 202 Loop to Exit 3. Right on E McDowell Road. Left on N 64th Street, right on E Indian School Road, left on N Scottsdale Road to destination | **Hours** Daily 9am – 7pm and by appointment | **Tip** Just down the street is Scottsdale Sidewalk Surfer, Arizona's first skateboard shop (2602 N Scottsdale Road, Scottsdale, www.sidewalksurfer.com).

85 Rare Crested Saguaro
Scientists baffled by cause of mutation

There's only one crested, or cristate, saguaro cactus at the Desert Botanical Garden, which speaks to its rareness and its uniqueness. The saguaro, with its classic "arms," is an icon for the American Southwest, as this cactus only grows in a portion of the Sonoran Desert, which covers southwestern Arizona, northwestern Mexico, and a tiny portion of southeast California.

Growing up to an average of 40 feet tall, the saguaro is also the largest cactus in North America. You've seen this magnificent botanical marvel in movies, in art, in advertising graphics, and even as an emoji on your smartphone. Saguaros bloom in the spring, and Arizonans are proud to call the stunning white blossoms the State Flower of Arizona.

According to the National Park Service, only one in 200,000 saguaros grows a crest. So although you may be tempted to think that if you've seen one crested saguaro you've seen them all, that would not at all be true, as every crest has a unique appearance. This mystery of the crest on top of these cacti continues to baffle lifelong desert dwellers, as well as the scientific community. Much research has been conducted on the saguaro, and speculation about this abnormality abounds. Because they grow so slowly, thorough research takes time. Some say it's caused by freeze damage, and some say it's lightning strikes, or poor soil conditions. Others say it's a genetic mutation, or perhaps hormones gone awry. Whatever it is, the crested structure is fascinating, beautiful, and mesmerizing.

The Desert Botanical Garden cares for nearly 4,500 species of plants and has more than 50,000 individual plants on display in its outdoor exhibits. In addition to the one crested saguaro, you'll find other native cacti here, including fishhook, prickly pear, and organ pipe cactus. The garden is a steward of more than 500 rare and endangered plant species.

Address 1201 N Galvin Parkway, Phoenix, AZ 85008, +1 (480) 941-1225, www.dbg.org, contact@dbg.org | **Getting there** Bus 56 to Desert Botanical Garden | **Hours** Oct–Apr daily 8am–8pm, May–Sep daily 7am–8pm | **Tip** Enjoy an easy hike communing with saguaro and other native cacti at Cave Creek Regional Park (37019 N Lava Lane, Cave Creek, www.maricopacountyparks.net/park-locator/cave-creek-regional-park).

86 Redwood Pipeline Scandal

First efforts in municipal water works had leaks

You would never know it today, but the lovely Verde Park in Garfield Historic District was the site of Phoenix's first waterworks, an enterprise that would end in scandal and leave the city wanting for water. As in the early years of many of today's major cities, water supply and water filtration were challenges for budding Phoenix. There were multiple options in the early 1900s for water delivery, one of which was the Phoenix Water Company. The company had drilled wells at the site of today's Verde Park in 1889, and the water was somewhat salty. Most of the city's 3,000 residents had been using untreated water for their household needs. In 1907, the city purchased Phoenix Water Company for $150,000.

Fast forward a few years and Phoenicians were anxious for better water, which Phoenix Water Company promised to deliver by tapping into the Verde River, nearly 30 miles away. More than $1 million dollars was earmarked for the water pipeline project, which ended up not being enough after the inflation caused by World War I. A pipeline was built, but not with metal or concrete. Instead, a wooden pipeline was constructed using redwood and metal barrel hoops (think wine barrel) after an out-of-state consulting engineer, William L. Church, gave assurances that the redwood would be "as permanent as any other material…and may be adopted by you without fear of disappointment," reported in the *Arizona Republic*. Over the next few years, people wanting water would knock holes in the pipeline, creating serious leaks. Eventually, the project failed. The wooden pipeline was fully replaced with concrete by 1931, at a substantial cost and after a substantial loss.

Today, Verde Park is a city park with a playground and shaded picnic tables. Is it safe to drink the water? Yes. And most people agree that the number one rule for enjoying the desert is to stay hydrated.

Address 916 E Van Buren Street, Phoenix, AZ 85006, +1 (602) 495-5109, www.phoenix.gov/parks | Getting there Bus 3 to Van Buren & 11th Streets | Hours Daily 5:30am–10pm | Tip Enjoy a juicy steak at Durant's, a dining destination where myths abound about politicians and other characters, and be sure to ask for the "Marilyn Monroe table." Walk in like a local: through the kitchen via the back door (2611 N Central Avenue, www.durantsaz.com).

87 Rosson House

Arizona's first bride lived here

The cornerstone of Heritage Square and Science Park in downtown Phoenix is the historic Rosson House, once the home of a young girl named Hazel Goldberg. She would grow up, fall in love, and become the first bride in the new State of Arizona. Hazel's engagement to Joseph Melczer was announced in the *Arizona Republic* in January 1912, stating that the two would marry in March that year, on a day to be announced. But one week later, they set the date for their wedding "on the birthday of the patron saint of all true lovers," Valentine's Day.

The story not told in the papers about the wedding celebrated that day was that Hazel and Joseph had been waiting for official word from the White House that Arizona had been granted statehood. The exciting news reached Phoenix via telegraph within 55 minutes, and the couple held their wedding on February 14, 1912. The ring bearer was three-year-old Barry Goldwater (1909–1998), future Senator of Arizona and presidential candidate in 1964.

The Rosson House, built in 1895 in the Queen Anne style with Eastlake decorative elements, is named for its original owners Dr. Roland and Flora Rosson, who lived here for only two years. The Goldbergs purchased it in 1897, and a flurry of other owners and residents would pass through its doors until the early 1970s, when it was rescued from the wrecking ball, thanks to the local community. The City of Phoenix purchased it, placed it on the National Register of Historic Places, and had it fully restored.

Today, you will discover numerous historic buildings and vibrant businesses nearby, including a James Beard Award-winning pizzeria, an enticing gift shop, a cozy welcome center, the 1980 Lath Pavilion, inspired by 19th-century conservatories, and the Arizona Science Center. Though Heritage Square is a popular destination for locals and tourists alike it holds many secrets to be discovered.

Address 113 N 6th Street, Phoenix, AZ 85004, +1 (602) 258-0048, heritagesquarephx.org |
Getting there Bus 1, 3, 7 to Van Buren & 7th Streets | Hours Unrestricted from outside,
see website for tour and event schedule | Tip Now that you have experienced 19th-century
Phoenix, head to walkable Arizona Center, where you will experience theatre, cinema, sushi,
donuts, splendid architecture, and a lovely park (455 N 3rd Street, www.arizonacenter.com).

88 Rustler's Rooste

Slide into a rattlesnake and cactus appetizer

As you drive up to Rustler's Rooste, look for a massive American flag flapping higher than anything in sight. And greeting you at the front door is a longhorn. Not a costumed mascot longhorn, but an actual bovine. His name is Horny.

The cavernous entrance is dark but sparkly with colorful lighting, and leads you to the hostess stand, where someone wearing an American-flag shirt greets you. Once it's time to go to your table, there's the exciting option of hopping on an actual slide down to the lower dining room. There's seating upstairs, too, but kids love the slide, as do many grownups. You're invited to embrace your childlike inhibitions here.

The daily live music at Rustler's Rooste is just the beginning of the entertainment. The adventurous menu, heaped with traditional Western dishes, makes this a uniquely Wild West experience. The most popular dish on the menu, or at the very least the most talked about, is only for the bravest of souls: the rattlesnake and cactus fries appetizer. Yes, it's real rattlesnake, and the fries are made from actual cactus. "Authentic" on this menu means the real thing here!

Phoenix has had a longtime love affair with rattlesnakes. The ridge-nosed rattlesnake has been the official State Reptile of Arizona since 1986. The Arizona Rattlers football team was founded in 1992, and the 2001 World Series Champion Diamondbacks debuted in 1998. The snake on your plate here is a diamondback. It's a seasonal dish, but there's always a memorable meal here for you.

Diners who do eat the rattlesnake appetizer receive a discount on a plush toy rattlesnake or an "I Ate the Snake" t-shirt at the well-stocked gift shop on the lower level. There are multiple opportunities to bring home a memory from Rustler's Rooste. And if the rattlesnake is a little too adventurous for you, maybe you can try something smaller like a scorpion lollipop.

Address 8383 S 48th Street, Phoenix, AZ 85044, +1 (602) 431-6474, www.rustlersrooste.com | Getting there By car, take I-10 to Exit 155 and go west on Baseline Road. Turn left onto Arizona Grand Parkway. Take the traffic circle exit onto Pointe Parkway W and follow it to S Pointe Parkway E. Take the first right, then left to S 48th Street | Hours Saloon: daily 4pm (closing times vary); steakhouse: Mon–Fri 5pm, Sat & Sun 4:30pm | Tip On Sundays, check out the vibrant Ahwatukee Farmers Market in Phoenix's southernmost neighborhood at the foothills of South Mountain (4700 E Warner Road, arizonacommunityfarmersmarkets.com/ahwatukee-farmers-market).

89 Samurai Comics
Bring the whole family

There's no shortage of comic book shops in Metro Phoenix. So, what makes Samurai Comics special? It's a comic treasure trove where you can bring your whole comic book-loving family – there's something here for everyone! At first glance, it all kind of melds together, but take your time to meander through the store, and you will find gem after gem after gem. Their tagline says it all: "We Sell Fun!"

On the shelves and racks are thousands of comics and more than 100,000 back issues just for the asking, as well as anime, manga, hardcover graphic novels, comic illustration collections, magazines, cookbooks, comic-themed lunch boxes, posters, model kits, puzzles, Funko Pops, and an army of statues and action figures.

There are lots of board games, too. Samurai Comics has hosted game nights since its founding in 2002, and they're going stronger than ever. It's a great way to make new friends and connect with the local community. Although sometimes competitive, these are the gaming people you've been looking for. For the youngsters, there are plushies, toys, stickers, Little Golden Books, and *Dog Man* graphic novels. And the "well-seasoned" shopper might enjoy some of the vintage comic books in the impressive collection that changes almost daily. Or choose to start with a whole new series. The friendly staff will be happy to help you make some selections based on your personal interests.

According to YouTube, in 2023 more than 80 percent of total views of videos related to anime came from countries outside of Japan. Samurai's owners Mike and Moryha met while working at another comic book shop, then dated, married, and opened their own store. In the beginning, Mike's favorite anime was *Rurouni Kenshin*, a series about the adventures of a young wandering swordsman. More than 20 years later, Samurai Comics is Arizona's largest chain of comic book specialty stores.

Address 1602 E Indian School Road, Phoenix, AZ 85016, +1 (602) 265-8886,
www.samuraicomics.com, phoenix@samuraicomics.com | Getting there Valley Metro
Light Rail north to Indian School / Central Avenue Station; bus 41 to destination | Hours
Mon, Tue, Thu, Sat 11am–6pm, Wed 9am–8pm, Fri 11am–7pm, Sun noon–5pm | Tip
Collectors Marketplace has collectibles ranging from vintage comics to toys, action figures,
and video games (4031 N 24th Street, www.collectorsmarketplace.com/home.html).

90 San Carlos Hotel Star Walk

Walk amongst the Hollywood stars…and ghosts?

Celebrating its 65th anniversary in 1993, the San Carlos Hotel offered free champagne tours of its historic gallery. On the N Central and W Monroe sidewalks, they also installed a Star Walk, with large golden stars bearing the names and signatures of Hollywood legends who had stayed at the hotel.

Among the many celebrities is Marilyn Monroe, who stayed here while filming *Bus Stop* (1956). She favored room 326 near the pool. Clark Gable and Carole Lombard reportedly spent many romantic nights together at the hotel. Other guests included Betty Grable, Ingrid Bergman, and Gary Cooper. Mae West stayed here while promoting *I'm No Angel* at the nearby Orpheum Theatre in 1929. And the original "Blonde Bombshell" Jean Harlow, who tragically died at the height of her career at only 26 years old, has a brightly shining star here too. Charles Harris is one of the least famous people with a star. He was actually one of the original owners and served as general manager. He and his family lived in a rooftop suite, and his widow sold the hotel in 1967.

On this site originally stood the city's first school, erected in 1874. The school closed in 1916 to make way for the new luxury hotel, which would open in just over a decade. It was the most modern hotel in the Southwest, the first high-rise hotel in Phoenix with air conditioning, and the first high-rise hotel in Arizona with hand-operated elevators.

Are there ghosts at the San Carlos? In 1928, a young woman named Leone Jensen, dressed in an evening gown, checked out of the hotel – from the roof. Some say that they have seen a "gauzy form of a woman" in the hotel's hallways. Others say they have heard three young schoolboys running through the hallways and laughing.

Address 202 N Central Avenue, Phoenix, AZ 85004, +1 (602) 253-4121, www.historichotelsancarlos.com, info@hotelsancarlos.com | Getting there Valley Metro Light Rail to Van Buren/Central Avenue; bus 542, 563, 575, GAL, I-10, I-17, SMW | Hours Unrestricted | Tip Tovrea Castle was originally a hotel built by an Italian hoping to create a community. The 1929 stock market crash dashed those dreams, but the "wedding cake" building remains a marvel to behold (5025 E Van Buren Street, www.visitphoenix.com/stories/post/touring-tovrea-castle).

91 Schreiner's Fine Sausages

It's bigger on the inside

This tiny little "sausage chalet" might look like a Bavarian roadside stand, but it's so much more. Positioned at a non-perpendicular angle on the street corner, this family-owned market offers more than 60 varieties of sausages, as well as mustards, sauerkrauts, pickles, spices, condiments, and other meats. They do their butchering in a non-attached building on the same property. If you've dined around Phoenix, you just might have enjoyed some of their high-quality sausages and meats at local restaurants. Many such dining destinations proudly note "Schreiner's" on their menus.

The company was founded in 1952 by Hugo Schreiner, and the products were made using recipes from Germany. The storefront opened in 1955. At age 13, Gary Schiller began working at Schreiner's on the weekends, and he would go on to purchase the business from Schreiner at the young age of 20. Schiller's future wife Nancy started working there while she was earning her degree in nutrition from Arizona State University. She later married the boss, but today, Nancy runs the business and always with a beaming smile, all these years later.

If you've ever watched *Dr. Who*, you will understand why Schreiner's is described as being "bigger on the inside." The shop looks quite small from the outside, but once you step inside, the wide variety of offerings here makes it seem gargantuan. Nancy has a big heart, too, welcoming customers in like she has known you for years, even if it's your first time shopping here.

While 7th Street is one of Phoenix's major thoroughfares and filled with exciting shopping, restaurants, bars, and fun things to do, this particular stretch is fairly nondescript. So while everything around the shop has changed, its exterior is the same charming design and the same red and white colors that it has been for more than 70 years. And the delicious sausages are still homemade.

Address 3601 N 7th Street, Phoenix, AZ 85014, +1 (602) 265-2939, www.schreinerssausage.com, schreinerssausage@gmail.com | **Getting there** Bus 7 to 7th Street & Weldon Avenue | **Hours** Wed – Sat 10am – 4pm | **Tip** Short Leash Hotdogs & Doughnuts features scratch-made brioche doughnuts and a plethora of hotdogs sourced locally from Schreiner's. This is a must-dine destination for an elevated hotdog experience, with a bar, pool table, and live music (4221 N 7th Avenue, www.shortleashhotdogs.com).

92 Scorpion Gulch

Trading post and a home near a gold mine

William J. Lunsford moved to Phoenix in 1911 with his bride Josephine after they were married in Louisiana, his home state. He worked as an engineer with Southern Pacific and Arizona Eastern Railroads. Some say that the gold mines on South Mountain brought him to this specific locale. There are indeed gold mines on South Mountain, though they're inactive and abandoned today. But it was actually his engineering expertise.

As a civil engineer, Lunsford was hired to train South Mountain's Civilian Conservation Corps (CCC), a Congress-established program for young, unemployed men during the Great Depression. In 1936, he decided to build a family home on land within walking distance to the entrance of South Mountain Park.

One of the buildings on the compound became the South Mountain Trading Post, today topped with a faded white sign that reads, "This is Scorpion Gulch." Lunsford liked the name so much, reportedly coined because of the abundance of scorpions in a nearby rainwater wash, that he copyrighted it. He never made money off the name, and the copyright was not renewed, but several businesses of the same era adopted "Scorpion Gulch" in their own names.

Lunsford collected stones from the area to build the trading post and the family home, which includes a castle turret. Today all that remains are the walls, steps, and a fireplace, a feature not always found in Phoenix homes. The Trading Post, separate from the home, is where Lunsford sold Native American jewelry, Indian "curios," leather goods, drinks, and snacks.

William and Josephine passed away in the 1960s and are interred at St. Francis Catholic Cemetery. They were survived by 12 grandchildren and six great grandchildren at the time. Today, you can explore their hand-built home at Scorpion Gulch, which is protected by the Phoenix Historic Property Register.

Address 10225 S Central Avenue, Phoenix, AZ 85042, www.phoenixwithkids.net/scorpion-gulch-in-phoenix | **Getting there** By car, follow S Central Avenue to destination | **Hours** Unrestricted | **Tip** Take the sting out of a scorpion photo-op with Tom Otterness's whimsical bronze sculptures collectively titled *Social Invertebrates*. A playful, human-size scorpion awaits your giant smile (Southwest corner of Washington Street & S 5th Street, www.tomotterness.net/artworks/social-invertebrates).

93 Sisters of Mercy

Memorial Wall chronicles a history of healing

Sisters of Mercy, established in the early 1800s in Dublin, Ireland, has an enduring legacy of care and compassion that has reached every corner of the planet, including Phoenix. When you arrive at the main entrance of St. Joseph's Hospital and Medical Center, you are only steps away from what sounds like a miraculous journey to create, facilitate, and build what is today a magnificent center of medical treatment, compassionate caregiving, and healing. It was Sister Catherine McAuley (1778–1841) who established the first House of Mercy in Dublin. By the time she passed away, fourteen Mercy houses had opened their doors.

Fast forward a number of years to the story of Sister M. Peter, who wanted to open a center in Phoenix for people suffering from tuberculosis. She did not accept "no" nor even "not right now" for an answer. With her determination and that of her five fellow sisters, the idea became a reality. In an 1895 article, the *Arizona Gazette* announced the opening of the Sisters' hospital, a six-room, brick house at 4th and Polk Streets. In the Arizona Center downtown, you can find a sculpture with five figures holding a sphere, titled, *It's in Your Hands* by Robert J. Miley, that marks the locale of the original hospital.

The hospital grew, of course, and is now St. Joseph's Hospital, which opened in 1953 on Thomas Road. The Mercy Memorial Wall, running both sides of the corridor just beyond the welcome desk here, chronicles the magnificent accomplishments of founder Sister McAuley through to the modern-day establishment of the world-renowned Barrow Neurological Institute, and beyond. The Memorial Wall marks the establishment of the first nursing school in Arizona (1910), Vice President Nixon's visit (1960s), First Lady Nancy Reagan's ribbon-cutting visit (1984), Pope John Paul II's visit (1987), and Muhammad Ali's ribbon-cutting visit (1990).

Address 350 W Thomas Road, Phoenix, AZ 85013, www.supportstjosephs.org/
sisters-of-mercy--st.-josephs-foundation | Getting there Bus 29 to Thomas Road &
5th Avenue | Hours Daily 5am–10pm | Tip Across the street is local favorite, family-
owned Maskadores Taco Shop. The made-from-scratch street tacos and the wet burrito
are delicious (53 W Thomas Road, www.maskadorestacoshops.com).

94 Sphinx Date Co.
A date night with a date shake and more dates

For a night out your sweetheart will not soon forget, bring them for a "date shake" at Sphinx Date Co. Palm & Pantry. These delicious shakes, made with Medjool dates, vanilla ice cream, and milk, are prepared on the spot by Rebecca and Sharyn Seitz, the daughter and mother team who own and operate the quaint and bountiful shop on the southern edge of Old Town Scottsdale.

They're the fourth family since 1951 to run the shop, and they are enthusiastic supporters of all things Phoenix- and Arizona-made. They are also steadfast stewards of the history of the 1920s Sphinx Date Ranch. Highly sought after for their creamy texture and delicate rich taste, the Black Sphinx dates are seasonally available. Medjool dates grown here in Arizona are available year round.

In partnership with the southwest Arcadia neighborhood Mount Grove, a small part of what was once the Sphinx Date Ranch and nearly lost to history, the Seitz's are able to secure the precious Black Sphinx dates September to October and share them with locals and visitors to the shop. There are approximately 300 Black Sphinx Date Palms in the Mount Grove neighborhood, home to nearly all of the remaining trees from the date ranch of a century ago.

The shop has a large, stone fountain at the entrance, lovely, street-facing patio seating, and private parking. Peruse the shop, and you will discover a cornucopia of Arizona products. For the extra-fun-loving, there is a selection of wines from vineyards throughout the state, which also come in gift boxes.

To go with your wine, there are selections of date gift boxes and trays, Arizona-made hot sauces, honey, pistachio, and pecans, and be sure to pick up some Ramona Farms products, too. Today grown in abundance by Ramona and Terry Button on the Gila River Indian Reservation, the tepary beans they farm were nearly lost to extinction. And remember to buy some extra dates for your date.

Address 3039 N Scottsdale Road, Scottsdale, AZ 85251, +1 (480) 941-2261, www.sphinxdateranch.com, info@sphinxdateranch.com | Getting there Bus 72 to Scottsdale Road & Earll Drive | Hours Mon–Sat 9am–5pm | Tip See where the Black Sphinx date palms grow in nearby Mount Grove (N 47th Street, north of the Arizona Canal).

95 Spielberg's Film Debut
An award-deserving 'red carpet' experience

The Phoenix Theatre Company commemorates being the site of Steven Spielberg's first feature film debut in 1964 with *Firelight,* a science-fiction adventure film that he produced and directed when he was 17 years old.

The full film has been lost to history – only 3 minutes and 40 seconds of it survive. But you can find clips on the internet. After watching even a few scenes from *Firelight*, you can easily see that the 1977 box-office hit *Close Encounters of the Third Kind* (1977) was inspired by the future Oscar winner's first movie. You'll notice that the title *Firelight* is in red letters, and the alien spaceship is represented by a large red orb, similar to one of the red lights representing the space aliens in *Close Encounters*.

On the wall just inside the theater entrance is a large image of Spielberg as we know him today, and a smaller image of a signed photograph of him looking up toward the then standalone Phoenix Little Theatre marquee. It is signed, "To P.L.T., My very first movie theatre." *Firelight* was shown here at 8pm on Wednesday, March 24, 1964. You could tell then that Spielberg had great aspirations, as he advertised the event as a "World Premiere." He worked at the Little Phoenix Theatre, now the Phoenix Theatre Company, and his father decided it would be perfect for his son's directorial debut. *Firelight* garnered a profit of $5, and it launched an unforgettable career.

When you arrive at the theatre, which is next door to the Phoenix Art Museum, you will see high-design, geometric squares and rectangles featuring large-format photographs of shows that have graced the stage here, as well as a big square with a red band around it, at the top of which reads, "Steven Spielberg Entrance." This entrance opens to a long corridor. On performance nights, it's flooded with red lights to create a "Red Carpet" experience for all patrons.

Address 1825 N Central Avenue, Phoenix, AZ 85004, +1 (602) 254-2151,
www.phoenixtheatre.com, info@phoenixtheatre.com | Getting there Valley Metro Light
Rail to McDowell / Central Avenue; bus 0 to Central Avenue & Palm Lane | Hours
Walkway: unrestricted; box office: Mon – Fri 10am – 5:30pm | Tip At the Phoenix Art
Museum next door, you can experience Yayoi Kusama's infinity mirror room in an exhibition
titled *You Who are Getting Obliterated in the Dancing Swarm of Fireflies* (1625 N Central
Avenue, www.phxart.org).

96   St. Mary's Basilica

Pope John Paul II prayed here

In 1985, His Holiness Pope John Paul II (1920–2005) proclaimed St. Mary's Basilica, officially The Church of the Immaculate Conception of the Blessed Virgin Mary, to be a minor basilica. The Ceremony of Designation was held on Sunday, December 8, 1985. Two years later, on Monday, September 14, 1987, the Pope knelt in prayer in the center aisle of the church during his only visit to Arizona. The prayer bench where he knelt is located today exactly next to the column in the church where he prayed, close to the main entrance near the back of the church. After his prayers, the Pope addressed an audience of thousands from the balcony.

Near the street in the grassy courtyard next to the church is a bronze statue of Pope John Paul II, reaching out to the masses, to commemorate his 1987 visit to Phoenix. Also on the grounds are statues of Saint Teresa of Calcutta (1910–1997), better known as Mother Teresa, and St. Francis of Assisi. This church is home to the largest collection of stained-glass windows in Arizona, and they're incredibly luminous and beautiful. The interior of the church has a cruciform layout. The top of the cross is at the main altar. In a tradition that goes back to the third century, a dome, this one in stained glass, is situated above the altar. Above the main entrance on Monroe Street is a large, spectacular rose window. The west and east transepts have windows depicting the victory of eternal life over death.

The Pope's 1987 visit was part of a nine-city tour of the United States. His visit included a parade down Central Avenue in the popemobile, a blessing from Emmett White, a Native American of the Pima tribe, who gave the Pope an eagle feather, and a visit to St. Joseph's Hospital on Thomas Road. In Tempe, he held a mass for 75,000 at Sun Devil Stadium. Pope John Paul II was canonized on Sunday, April 27, 2014, and became St. John Paul II.

Address 231 N 3rd Street, Phoenix, AZ 85004, +1 (602) 354-2100,
www.saintmarysbasilica.org, frontdesk@smbphx.org | Getting there Valley Metro Light
Rail to Van Buren/Central Avenue; bus 1, 3, 7, SME, SR51 to Van Buren & 3rd Streets |
Hours Unrestricted from outside | Tip You can see the Papal Cross that was at Sun Devil
Stadium during mass with Pope John Paul II at Catholic Cathedral of Saints Simon and
Jude. The Pope also visited this cathedral, as did Mother Teresa (6351 North 27th Avenue,
www.simonjude.org).

97 __ Stardust Pinbar

Walk-in cooler door is a pinball rabbit hole

When Alice fell through the rabbit hole, she tumbled into Wonderland. When you're at Ziggy's Magic Pizza Shop, standing at the unassuming, small order window, you might not realize that there's a wonderland on the other side of the silver, walk-in cooler door. Is it a speakeasy? Well, you do have to know where you're going, and they do have adult beverages. So, in a sense, yes, Stardust Pinbar is a speakeasy – and a pinball destination. If you know glam rock's Ziggy Stardust (Starman David Bowie's stage name 1972–1973), then you totally get the naming of this magical place. And the pizza is pretty amazing, too.

There is some patio seating with red and white striped metal umbrellas to shade you from the scalding Phoenix summer sun, but why sit outside when there's a giant disco ball calling your name? Walk through the silver cooler door, and the first thing you'll see is a multi-color, constantly changing, light-up dancefloor. You have arrived, and the fun has already commenced. Or will you be the one who brings it? Whichever it is, the staff in the pinbar will gladly bring you the same pizza offered at the front. They also serve wings and sandwiches, but definitely enjoy some delicious Ziggy's pizza. And the bartender will be happy to bring you the adult beverage(s) of your choosing, whether it be draft beer, a craft cocktail, shots, or a selection from their whiskey program.

You will find the walls adorned with the playfields of all genres of old pinball machines, with holes where there were once bumpers, bashtoys, and flippers. There are posters and photos of the "Starman" himself, as well as a giant neon lightning bolt behind the bar. It's not a *Harry Potter* reference – it's a Ziggy Stardust reference. And yes, there are indeed pinball machines, so play to your heart's content. Then heed the Grammy-award winner's call to the dance floor and "let's dance."

Address 401 W Van Buren Street, Phoenix, AZ 85003, +1 (602) 354-3004,
https://stardustpinbar.com | Getting there Bus 3, 6 to Van Buren & 5th Streets | Hours Sun
noon–midnight, Mon–Thu 5pm–midnight, Fri 5pm–2am, Sat noon–2am | Tip Local
artist Maggie Keane showcases the many looks of 'Ziggy Stardust' in her Bowie Tribute
Mural (1715 N 7th Street, www.instagram.com/maggiekeanezart).

98__ The Sun Worshipper
A landmark returns decades later

Once gracing the entrance of Park Central Mall, Phoenix's first suburban shopping mall, *The Sun Worshipper* sculpture was almost chucked into the scrap pile but was fortunately rescued and purchased by a local for the cost of hauling it away. Years later, it has been returned to the refurbished mall, where it resides on the other side of the property. The towering, 19-foot, 1,800-pound sculpture depicts a Native American person dressed in a loincloth with his arms and face pointing towards the sky. Back in the day, and even now, *The Sun Worshipper* makes a fantastic photo companion.

The sculptor was Dr. Walter K. Emory of Phoenix, who gave up his medical practice in 1964 to become a fulltime sculptor. He fashioned *The Sun Worshipper* in his own front yard on E Bethany Home Road in 1967, the same year it was placed at Park Central. It's made from scraps of welded steel and is copper in color, perhaps a nod to Arizona being the largest producer of copper in the United States. Emory passed away in 1975 at only 45 years old.

Originally opened in 1957, Park Central Mall, the shopping destination that was then on the outskirts of town, was built in the Mid-Century Modern style that is recognizable here today, along with some Postmodern updates. Most of the original buildings still stand. Charlie Sands, who rescued *The Sun Worshipper*, owned several businesses at Park Central. He ended up displaying the sculpture in his front yard for many years. Evidently, this work of art has an affinity for yards.

Some scoffed that this magnificent sculpture was not returned to its original location on the east side of the mall, but others saw it as a good sign, as the sculpture is seemingly offering up hope and well wishes to those finding themselves in St. Joseph's Hospital and Medical Center, Phoenix's first hospital, originally founded by the Sisters of Mercy in 1895.

Address 3121 N 3rd Avenue, Phoenix, AZ 85013, www.phoenixnewtimes.com/arts/under-the-sun-the-sun-worshipper-returns-park-central-11306623 | Getting there Valley Metro Light Rail to Thomas/Central Avenue; bus 0 to Central Avenue & Earll Drive | Hours Unrestricted | Tip The Green Woodpecker offers beer, tacos, and complimentary chips and salsa and is also located at Park Central Mall (3110 N Central Avenue, Suite 185, www.thegreenwoodpecker.com).

99 Susan Arreola Postcard Collection

Time travel through 2,500 vintage postcards

The lost art of written correspondence, especially via postcard, has not been wholly lost to history. There is a collection of vintage postcards – approximately 2,500 of them – in the Arizona Room at the Burton Barr Central Library, the city's main branch in the public library system. The Arizona Room is dedicated to the history and people of the state, and these fascinating postcards, a gift from the collection's namesake Susan Arreola, pictorially chronicle Phoenix's history from around the time that Arizona gained statehood in 1912 through the 1960s.

You can read as many as you want, and you really should because there's no other sensation like the satisfaction of perusing old photos, in this case postcards, to get a magical sense of the passage of time, to learn of things long forgotten, and to discover tidbits about your own city. Arreola started her collection in the 1990s, and it had grown to more than 12,000 by 2018, which is when she donated the first 2,500. The images and etchings on the postcards range from aerial shots to parks and hotels to resorts, and some are quite humorous.

Writing postcards has been likened to today's social media, which is indeed an accurate comparison, except perhaps for the speed of sharing. Postcards were, of course, delivered by the postal services of the world and not the internet, which would show up after the postmark date on any of the beautiful specimens here. Some of these postcards were never mailed, rather kept as a traveler's souvenir, and others with notes to friends and loved ones would be later collected by Arreola and her husband Daniel at their destinations around the country.

The Arizona Room, on the library's second floor, also holds a wide variety of artifacts, maps, magazines, and newspapers, including some Native American newspapers, such as the *Fort Apache Scout*, *Ak-Chin O'odham Runner*, and *Navajo Times*.

Address 1221 N Central Avenue, Phoenix, AZ 85004, +1 (602) 262-4636, www.phoenixpubliclibrary.org/Locations/BurtonBarr | Getting there Valley Metro Light Rail to McDowell / Central Avenue | Hours Mon 9am – 5pm, Tue – Thu 9am – 7pm, Fri & Sat 9am – 5pm, Sun 1 – 5pm | Tip Keep the vintage vibe going by heading over to Modern Manor, a "vintage-modern" furniture shop, where you can also enjoy Valentine, a full-service restaurant and full bar – also a popular brunch destination (4130 N 7th Avenue, www.modernmanorphx.com).

100 __ Thunderbird Field No. 1
Funded by Hollywood, future WWII pilots trained here

Where the campus of Arizona Christian University (ACU) sits today has a legacy of education. The site's history dates back to the early 1940s, when it served as a primary flight school during World War II. More than 10,000 young men entered training at what was originally called Thunderbird Field. Men and women from across the country worked on the school's aircraft and support services to keep the pilots and planes flying 24/7.

You can see three of the buildings from the original airfield/training school that remain today. The gem is the historic Air Control Tower and officers' quarters building, opened in 1941. You can't miss the visual control room, with its floor-to-ceiling glass windows and a red-orange windsock. Photos of it are best taken when there's a slight breeze engaging the windsock.

The other original buildings include the Thunderbird Field Administration Offices, today called Founder's Fieldhouse, and one of the four original hangars. American, British, Canadian, and Chinese pilots trained here during World War II.

As early as the late 1930s, there were those who sensed that war was coming. Among those were the founders of Southwest Airways (not affiliated with today's Southwest Airlines) Leyland Hayward, Hollywood producer and on the Executive Committee at TWA, and Jack Conolly, an experienced military pilot and aviation engineering inspector. According to Susan Johnson, ACU Historian and Associate Professor, Hayward's friends and clients purchased shares in the company, including Henry Fonda, Robert Taylor, and Janet Gaynor, as well as Oscar-winner Jimmy Stewart. Stewart was later drafted, became a bomber pilot, flew 20 combat missions, and retired with the rank of Brigadier General, the highest rank ever achieved by a Hollywood star. Stewart would go on to be awarded the Distinguished Flying Cross, as were Clark Gable and Gene Roddenberry.

Address 1 W Firestorm Way, Glendale, AZ 85306, +1 (800) 247-2697,
www.arizonachristian.edu, info@arizonachristian.edu | Getting there By car, take I-10 west
to I-17 north. Turn left on W Greenway Road, and then left on N 57th Avenue | Hours
Unrestricted. Required check-in at the front desk in the Administration Building | Tip
Thunderbird Lounge takes retro to the next and the coolest level (710 W Montecito
Avenue, https://thunderbirdloungephx.com).

101 Tonto Hills Kachina

The world's largest kachina doll

Standing sentry over the Tonto Hills subdivision in Cave Creek, directly northeast of Phoenix and west of Tonto National Forest, is a 39-foot-tall kachina doll – the world's largest. If you've spent any time in the Southwest, you have likely seen these dolls, but their cultural significance is not often shared.

Made by the Hopi peoples, kachina dolls are figures typically carved from cottonwood root to instruct young girls and new brides about *katsinas* or *katsinam*, the immortal beings that bring rain, control other aspects of the natural world and society, and act as messengers between humans and the spirit world. E. V. Graham, the Tonto Hills subdivision's developer, had this kachina doll built to induce his wife to move onto the property, which at that time, around 1970, was far out in the country. Carl Ludlow was the engineer for the project. The colossal doll is owned and maintained by the Tonto Hills Volunteer Fire Department right next door on N La Plata Road.

The structure is composed of nine concrete sections that were individually molded and then cast in Phoenix. The four lower sections are solid, and the upper sections are hollow but made of six-inch walls reinforced by steel. Designer Phillip Sanderson modeled the original kachina from clay and used authentic Hopi colors of turquoise, red, white, grey, and black.

Visit on a sunny day, easy to do in Phoenix, to see the full vibrance of this magnificent work of art. There's not a lot around the site, nor is there a discernible entrance, so you should have some excellent photo opportunities. This kachina doll represents a Corn Maiden Dancer kachina, who purifies the women who grind the corn for ceremonies. Painted on the base are traditional Hopi vegetables, accurately indicating the four points of the compass. The bean pod points north, the ear of corn south, and the watermelon and squash east and west.

Address 42026 N La Plata Road, Cave Creek, AZ 85331 | **Getting there** By car, take AZ-101 to N Pima Road then drive north, turn onto E Cave Creek Road going northeast, left onto N Old Mine Road, and right onto N la Plata Road | **Hours** Unrestricted | **Tip** Visit Sears-Kay Ruin nearby, which are magnificent architectural remnants of Native American culture that predate Christopher Columbus' arrival by 300 years (end of N Sears-Kay Ruin Road, www.fs.usda.gov/recarea/tonto/recarea/?recid=35235).

102 Tony DeMarco's Living Room

Once a "champion" piano bar

On the southeast corner of Camelback Road and 40th Street is a U-Haul rental shop that was once Tony DeMarco's Living Room, a highly successful piano bar and lounge. One of the last "neighborhood saloons" of that era, it was especially popular with Boston transplants and visitors from Boston. The owner of the U-Haul shop sponsored a larger-than-life photo of Tony DeMarco at the height of his career, on the side of the rectangular, white-block building, and an accompanying commemorative plaque with Tony's image and highlights of his fame. Tony DeMarco was a 1955 World Welterweight Champion and a 2019 inductee into the International Boxing Hall of Fame.

The son of Sicilian immigrants, he was born Leonardo Liotta – nicknamed "Nardo" – in Boston, Massachusetts, where he fought the vast majority of his career fights. At 15 years old, he borrowed a friend's baptismal certificate to get a birth certificate so that he could get boxing lessons as an amateur. That friend's name was Tony DeMarco, who was 18. Already successful at that point, DeMarco went pro at the age of 16.

Despite being a champion, he saw his share of losses. He and his wife moved their family to Phoenix, hoping it would help their son's asthma. Sadly, 14-year-old Vincent was riding his bike on Father's Day and got fatally struck by a car. The DeMarcos would later move back to Boston, where Tony was a boxing mentor and contributed his time to charitable causes.

Tony DeMarco visited Phoenix in his later years and got to see this tribute to his worldwide fame and the former bar. He mentioned in an interview that he knew nothing about the photo on the building or plaque, but that he was flattered and grateful for the recognition. DeMarco was always humble.

Address 4929 N 40th Street, Phoenix, AZ 85018 | Getting there By car, take 202 Loop east to N 44th Street exit. Drive north to E Camelback Road, turn left, and continue to N 40th Street | Hours Unrestricted | Tip Forno 301 is a total knockout for Sicilian pizza. This restaurant, bar, and pizzeria has a limited menu but is sure to please your pizza cravings (1616 N Central Avenue, www.forno301.com).

103__ *Tribute to Navajo Code Talkers*

The unbreakable code during World War II

More than 44,000 Native Americans fought for the United States in World War II. Over 400 of them were the now historic and celebrated Navajo Code Talkers, and they participated in every major conflict in the Pacific Theater from 1942 through the end of the war. Originally, 29 Navajo men enlisted, knowing only that they were going to communications school. They would create a unique code that was instrumental in winning numerous battles. Confusing and unbreakable by the Japanese, the code was actually Navajo, their complex, unwritten, native tongue.

The first permanent monument to the Navajo Code Talkers in the nation is here in Phoenix. It depicts a 10-foot-high, seated Navajo man with a flute. Representing the Code Talkers' communications radio, the flute in this sculptural tribute is used to symbolize the end of war and the coming of peace.

These soldiers' contributions to the US war efforts were classified until 1968. The sculpture was unveiled on March 2, 1989, at the then new Phoenix Plaza. It was sculpted by Doug Hyde who is of Native American descent from the Nez Perce, Assiniboine, and Chippewa tribes. He has works in the permanent collections at the Smithsonian Institution, the Heard Museum in Phoenix, and many others, including the Museum of Indian Arts and Culture in Santa Fe, where he has resided since 1972.

Major Howard Connor, 5th Marine Division signal officer, had six Navajo Code Talkers, also known as "Windtalkers," working 24 hours a day for the first two days of the battle at Iwo Jima. These six sent and received more than 800 messages in that time without errors. Connor is attributed as saying, "Were it not for the Navajos, the Marines would never have taken Iwo Jima."

Address 2901 N Central Avenue, Phoenix, AZ 85012 | **Getting there** Valley Metro Light Rail to Thomas/Central Avenue; bus 0, 29 to Central Avenue & Thomas Road | **Hours** Unrestricted | **Tip** A 2008 statue dedicated to the Navajo Code Talkers is located in Wesley Bolin Memorial Plaza alongside other war memorials. This sculpture depicts a Navajo Code Talker on a radio and in US military uniform (1700 W Washington Street).

104__Uptown Farmers Market
Local food, local crafts, and lots of locals

When you hear "farmer," you might think of people who live and work miles and miles from each other, shut off from those they feed. Here at Uptown Farmers Market, though, there is a strong sense of community. Many of the vendors, farmers and otherwise, are familiar with their fellow vendors and eagerly share news about everything available that day at this longtime, popular market, which draws an eclectic audience.

It's almost like going to a county fair. Kids can enjoy a bouncy house, face-painting, and treats. For your four-legged friends, there are doggie treats and even a bakery dedicated to canine culinary creations. The market is accurately billed as a gathering place with nearly 200 Arizona producers.

It's easy to find this market, and it's even easier to find parking nearby, a rarity in certain parts of the city. Once you're here, grab a cup of locally roasted coffee and a freshly baked pastry, and then you're ready for a pleasant, wholesome shopping experience. This market truly embraces an "all are welcome" approach. You will find young adults, the more seasoned shopper, people shopping for a home-cooked, date-night meal, or those seeking breakfast after a romantic date night. Beyond the farm-fresh produce, shoppers will find chocolates, flowers, plants, honey, eggs, herbs, jewelry, clothes, crafts, and even a few selections for carnivores.

Among the vendors are Amadio Ranch for honey, jam, preserves, and some of the best baked pies you've ever had in your life. Try the apple or strawberry-rhubarb. Fairy Godmother Baking Company sells excellent artisan bread, fresh cookies, and assorted nuts, warmed on site. And Bene Vivendo offers edible flowers, vegetables, fruits, herbs, and bouquets of fresh flowers. Keep in mind that it will take a little time to prepare your fresh dinner ingredients, so enjoy lunch at one of the multiple local food trucks.

Address 5757 N Central Avenue, Phoenix, AZ 85012, +1 (602) 859-5648, www.uptownmarketaz.com, info@uptownmarketaz.com | Getting there Bus 0 to Central & Montebello Avenues | Hours See website for seasonal hours | Tip Downtown Farmers Market is an oasis nestled within the skyscrapers of downtown Phoenix, easily accessible by walking or Valley Metro light rail (720 N 5th Street, www.downtownphoenixfarmersmarket.org).

105 __ USS *Arizona* Anchor
Heavy on the hearts of her visitors

It wouldn't take you long to figure out what you're seeing if you hap-pened upon an anchor weighing nearly 20,000 pounds, a soaring ship mast with flapping flags, and two battleship gun barrels. Only min-utes west of downtown Phoenix, one of the three anchors from the USS *Arizona* is situated in a place of honor and memorial at the top of Wesley Bolin Memorial Plaza in front of the Arizona State Cap-itol complex. Part of the Legislative Governmental Mall, the Plaza is fashioned after the National Mall in Washington, DC.

If you've been to Honolulu, Hawaii, you've probably paid hom-age at Pearl Harbor, where the USS *Arizona* lies at the bottom of the ocean, near Ford Island. Here in Phoenix, you can actually find numerous elements from that ill-fated ship. The anchor is on an ele-vated platform on which are engraved the names of the men who died in the attack. There are nine blue, steel pillars in the shape of a ship's hull that bear the names of the 1,902 Arizonans killed in World War II. The mast is located 1,177 feet away from the dome of the Capitol building – now a museum – which is symbolic of the 1,177 sailors and marines who perished on the USS *Arizona* on December 7, 1941.

It's highly fitting that Phoenix is home to such a revered artifact of remembrance, not only because Arizona is the namesake of the Pennsylvania-class battleship (commissioned in 1916, only four years after Arizona achieved statehood), but also because the state suffered the fourth highest number of casualties at Pearl Harbor after New Jersey, Oklahoma, and Hawaii. The USS *Arizona* Memorial was ded-icated on December 7, 1976. Sealed at that moment was a time cap-sule, located near the base of the anchor, which contains the names of the contributors and donors who made this memorial possible. The time capsule is to be opened on July 4, 2076, a few months before the memorial's 100th anniversary.

Address 1616 W Washington Street, Phoenix, AZ 85007, www.wesleybolinplaza.com | Getting there Bus DASH, GAL, I-10, SME, SMW, SR 51, 514, 521, 522, 531, 533, 535, 542, 562, 563, 571,573, 575 to W Washington Street & 15th Avenue | Hours Unrestricted | Tip Featuring a relic of the USS *Arizona* boathouse in Pearl Harbor, the USS *Arizona* Memorial Gardens showcases a series of vertical, illuminated tubes that outline the shape of the ill-fated battleship (7455 N Pima Road, Scottsdale, www.discoversaltriver.com/uss-arizona-memorial-gardens-at-salt-river).

106 Valley Youth Theatre

Emma Stone performed in 16 productions here

Academy Award winner Emma Stone, born in neighboring Scottsdale, began acting at 11 years old. Her earliest performances included 16 productions with Valley Youth Theatre (YVT) in downtown Phoenix. Other fantastic celebrities also performed at Valley Youth Theatre in their early years, including *American Idol* Season 6 winner Jordin Sparks; stage, television, and film star Kimiko Glenn; Phoenix native Sam Primack; singer and actress Chelsea Kane; actor, writer, producer Max Crumm; Broadway star Nick Cartell; and *Kyle XY* star Matt Dallas.

While at Valley Youth, Stone, then billed as Emily Stone, was in a production of *The Wiz* with fellow VYT alums Jordin Sparks, Max Crum, and Chelsea Staub. Sparks was never cast in a leading role while at VYT, but that was a consideration of her age, not her even-then obvious talent. In a familiar story, Matt Dallas was brought to VYT by his grandmother to see a show. That experience sparked his love of theatre, which eventually launched his career as an actor.

Bobb Cooper founded Valley Youth Theatre 1989. The mother of an auditioning child, Hope Ozer came aboard later and helped form a board of directors composed of local business leaders and professionals, who would champion the fledgling theatre.

VYT is no ordinary children's theatre. You'll find here a 30-foot-wide proscenium stage with an orchestra pit, scene and costume shops, rehearsal studios, and dressing rooms. The stardom that has been generated from these boards is remarkable and uncommon. Since its founding, VYT proudly and correctly touts that it has launched the careers of Broadway stars, an Academy Award winner, Grammy Award nominees, and television and film actors. The best role you might play at Valley Youth Theatre? At a place like this, where you can see outstanding children's shows for audiences of all ages, that would be the starring role of patron.

Address 525 N 1st Street, Phoenix, AZ 85004, +1 (602) 253-8188, www.vyt.com, boxoffice@vyt.com | Getting there Valley Metro Light Rail to Van Buren/Central Avenue; bus 7 to Fillmore Street & Central Avenue or Fillmore Street & 3rd Street | Hours See website for performance times | Tip Tee Pee Mexican Food is a favorite of Phoenix-born Lynda Carter of *Wonder Woman* fame. You will find the walls filled with autographed photos of performers, actors, a wide range of celebrities, athletes, presidents, and more (4144 E Indian School Road, www.teepeemexicanfood.com).

107 — *Water Mark*
Enchanting, gigantic, equine gargoyles

Just north of the Arizona Canal, as you're driving along E Indian Bend Road and happen to glance up from the road, you will be delighted by the sight of *Water Mark*. Five gigantic horse gargoyles gallop forth from plinths of dark gray, horizontal slabs and atop unstained concrete pedestals. They're situated on the north hillside of Indian Bend Wash, which is connected to the Palm Course of McCormick Ranch Golf Club, so you may even see a few golf carts whizzing by. While viewing these majestic creatures from a passing vehicle is exciting, actually walking up to them is a glorious experience.

Placed 125 feet apart in a row facing the road, overlooking the bridge underpass and the wash basin, the gargoyles stand a majestic 14 feet high. Look closely, and you will see that each have a different pose, giving the illusion of movement. Even their ears point in different directions. During and after heavy rains and flash floods, the gargoyles, like most gargoyles of a much smaller stature, redirect water into the wash through their mouths. Why horses, you ask? The gargoyles were a response to local flooding and a nod to the McCormick Arabian Ranch, once located nearby. Artists Laura Haddad and Tom Drugan created the design, and CWDC Fabrication made each sculpture out of more than 50 sheets of aluminum and over seven miles of welding stick.

The Indian Bend Wash Path is frequented by local walkers, runners, and cyclists, as well as photographers and art lovers. It's the perfect place to find fascinating discoveries while exploring Metro Phoenix. As you face the sculptures, you'll be standing between them and the bridge. On the base of the first one on the left are instructions on how to enjoy a virtual reality (VR) experience. Completed and installed in 2010, the *Water Mark* gargoyles continue to be steadfast in their sentinel duties and in delighting passersby.

Address 7605 E Indian Bend Road, Scottsdale, AZ 85250 | Getting there By car, take 101-Loop to E Indian Bend Road exit and travel west to the destination | Hours Unrestricted | Tip Also commissioned by Scottsdale Public Art, *Knight Rise* is a must-see, must-experience, walk-into sculpture by Arizona-based artist James Turrell on display at the Scottsdale Museum of Contemporary Art (7374 E 2nd Street, Scottsdale, www.smoca.org).

108__ West Wind Drive-In
Date Night old school style, but modern

Americana at its finest, West Wind Drive-In Glendale is the only such theatre in Arizona. In the 1950s, there were approximately 4,000 drive-ins around the country, but today there are only about 300. Some states have none at all now.

The classic drive-in experience started in 1933 on the evening of Tuesday, June 6, when Richard Hollingshead (1899–1975) opened the world's first drive-in cinema in Pennsauken Township, New Jersey. It would become a popular pastime and exponentially growing industry in the 1940s with the advent of the 'squawk box,' the wired speaker that moviegoers would hang on the interior side of their car windows to hear the soundtrack.

Today's West Wind Drive-Ins are family-owned, and have been since they first opened in the 1950s. For movie buffs and those seeking a unique date night or a fun, affordable family outing, the drive-ins have adopted the latest in cinema technology, featuring all-digital projectors.

West Wind shows first-run movies at the same time as indoor theatres, surprisingly. They also offer discounts through a membership program, and special events, including free and discounted movie nights. As if an awesome movie experience wasn't enough, they also host the weekly Glendale Market, where treasure-seekers will discover rows and rows of bargains and fresh produce.

Bring your lawn chairs, your frisbees, and your love of movies for this nearly lost Americana experience. At the snack bar, you will find high-quality brands and products. The popcorn is Orville Redenbacher, hotdogs are Nathan's Famous, the pizza is fresh from the oven, and quesadillas are made to order. Wash it all down with a fountain drink or stave off the Arizona heat with a classic ICEE. Mixing an old-school atmosphere with the latest digital technology, West Wind creates the ultimate drive-in experience of yesteryear for today.

Address 5650 N 55th Avenue, Glendale, AZ 85301, +1 (623) 939-9715, www.westwinddi.com/locations/glendale | **Getting there** By car, take 101-Loop to W Bethany Home Road exit and drive east to N 55th Avenue | **Hours** See website for movie schedule | **Tip** Have a sweet tooth after all that delicious salty popcorn? Head over to Old Town Candy & Toys for a vast array of old-fashion candy and some rather unique toys (4000 N Scottsdale Road, Scottsdale, www.oldtowncandyandtoys.com).

109 Whisked Away Cooking School

A reluctant cook becomes a chef and teacher

Near Old Cross-Cut Canal Park in the Arcadia Osborn neighborhood is a lovely, mid-century, ranch home that also happens to be a cooking school. In the front yard is a gigantic rosemary bush, a symbol with many meanings since ancient times, including good luck. The herb is also known for having healing properties, enhancing memory, and for elevating moods. And your mood will improve as you enter Maggie Norris' home on Mulberry Drive, also known as Whisked Away Cooking School.

Years ago, Norris would help her mother with her catering business, but it wasn't for her. Instead, she went to Vanderbilt University, where she graduated in 1998. A few years later, she received a cooking class as a gift. That experience became an epiphany, one that led to the pursuit of a culinary career, and one where she would fall in love with sharing her rekindled love of all things culinary with friends new and old. She attended Scottsdale Culinary Institute and grew skills exponentially. As fortune would have it, the 2011 Arizona Cottage Food Law allows for Norris' Whisked Away Cooking School to be operated from her home, an infrequently availed opportunity to make this cooking school a lovely and useful experience for her students.

What makes it all wholly unique is Norris' own experience. She worked at the Food Network in New York with world-class chefs, including Cat Cora, Rocco DiSpirito, and Sara Moulton, to name a few. When she returned to Phoenix, she was a regional chef for an appliance brand and worked in sales. In 2009, her friends asked her to give them a cooking class, which was the birth of Whisked Away, where she now teaches classes for eight on knife skills, cooking basics, and kitchen safety, all in an environment that fosters camaraderie and fun.

Address 4823 E Mulberry Drive, Phoenix, AZ 85018, +1 (480) 330-6525, www.whiskedaway.net | Getting there By car, from I-10 take the exit onto the 202-Loop, then take the exit onto 143 North. Turn right onto McDowell Road, left onto N 48th Street, right onto E Osborn Road, right onto N 50th Street, and right onto Mulberry Drive | Hours See website for class schedule | Tip Sweet Basil Culinary Center in Scottsdale is an all-in-one destination for entertaining supplies, cooking tools, and recreational cooking classes (8900 E Pinnacle Peak Road, Scottsdale, sweetbasilgourmet.com).

110 __ Wide World Maps & MORE!

Largest map store in the Southwest

Blink, and you'll miss it. Fortunately for cartography lovers, there's an assortment of globes in the front windows of Wide World Maps & MORE to grab your attention. Inside is a wonderfully delightful collection of maps about and from all corners of the globe, from Tempe to Timbuktu. You'll find street atlases, wall maps, road maps, topography maps, GPS units, map software, and map accessories, as well as travel-related books and gift items.

As you look around, you may get a sense of cartography overload, as the walls are filled with maps. But you will quickly see that the shop is logically categorized. In the far left are travel maps, the kind that you might have carried in your car prior to GPS apps. These are often filled with travel tidbits that you just don't get on your phone or automobile's navigation system. They can also serve as a quick tutorial in the still-important skill of map reading. One side of this area has maps for the Southwest's states and cities. Another has maps for areas in Mexico and South America, and a third set of racks has maps of cities around the world. You're covered from the Grand Canyon to Germany.

There are driving maps, hiking maps, hunting maps, and even a few flat-Earth maps. You might also spot some local maps that were produced at this very location. Within these walls is a laminating shop and a busy online-order fulfillment operation, but there's nothing quite like shopping in person for a special map. If you have always wanted your very own globe, there is a selection here that ranges from the classic classroom globe to a grown-up globe that opens up to reveal a bar. The happy hour that seems a world away is at your fingertips. Robert Molner (1932–2017) and James Willinger opened Wide World Maps & MORE in 1975. Stop by and lose yourself in a world of maps that will help you find your way.

Address 2133 E Indian School Road, Phoenix, AZ 85016, +1 (602) 279-2323, www.maps4u.com | **Getting there** By car, take I-10 to SR 51 North, then take the exit onto E Indian School Road east | **Hours** Mon–Fri 10am–5pm | **Tip** Stop by the Phoenix Visitor Center on the sixth floor of the One Arizona Center building for maps, brochures, and in-person information about the fifth-largest city in the country (400 E Van Buren Street, www.visitphoenix.com/visitor-center).

111 Xeriscape Garden

Gardening possibilities in low-water spaces

You may have heard it called "zero-scape," but the water-efficient, environmentally appropriate landscape design is actually called "xeriscape," and it's a rising trend in Metro Phoenix. It's also a great way to avoid gardening and mowing the grass.

Glendale Xeriscape Demonstration Garden, initially began in 1990 behind the Glendale Public Library Main Library, features more than 400 species of low-water, desert plants, including a succulent garden, a variety of cactus, and other heat-tolerant flora, all on nearly four acres of land. Look for saguaro, especially when they're in bloom in the springtime, as well as hummingbirds, lizards, butterflies, and the bright pink flowers of the Baja Fairy Duster plant. You might also see a number of other animals including visiting peacocks from neighboring Sahuaro Historic Ranch. Look for plant and tree labels with common and botanical names listed and make a note of the ones you like.

At first glance, this demonstration garden shows just how lush and inviting a low-water-use garden can be. You can find something in bloom here any time of the year. There is ample seating, including some benches covered in thriving, low-water desert plants, and shade trees. There are numerous works of art here, too, like the blue sphere made with found glass. Placards throughout teach you about planting and maintaining a xeriscape garden, which benefits the environment and also saves you time and money. You may find useful advice on how to plan irrigation for your garden. And you may learn new strategies around water conservation in general, always a topic of great interest in Phoenix.

The library itself offers classes and events, including gaming, astronomy, virtual reality, story time, and reading challenges. And of course, they have numerous books on life in the Sonoran Desert, low-water gardening, and conservation.

Address 5959 W Brown Street, Glendale, AZ 85302, www.glendaleaz.com/Live/
City_Services/Water_Services/Water_Conservation_and_Sustainable_Living/
xeriscape_demonstration_garden | Getting there Bus GUS, 59 to 59th Avenue & Brown
Street | Hours Daily dawn–dusk | Tip Nearby Westgate Entertainment District offers
wintertime ice skating, a giant splash pad for kids in warmer weather, and the beautiful
Waterdance Plaza (6770 N Sunrise Boulevard, Glendale, www.westgateaz.com).

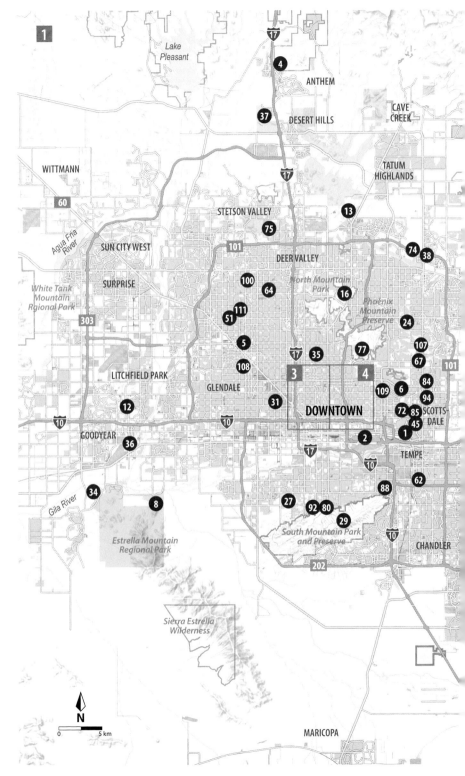

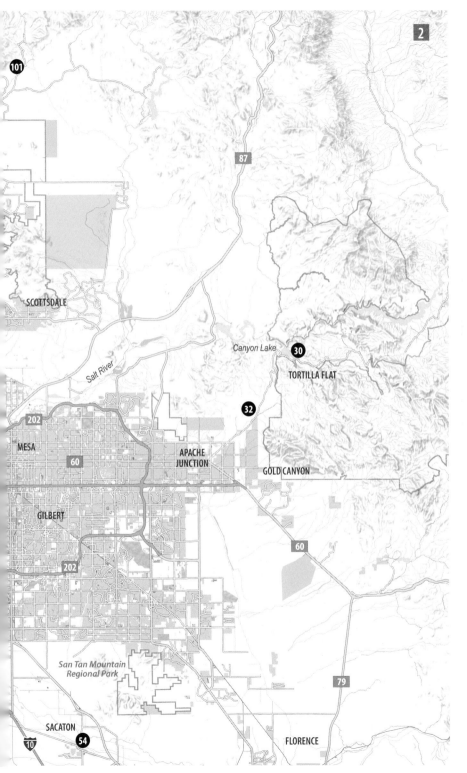

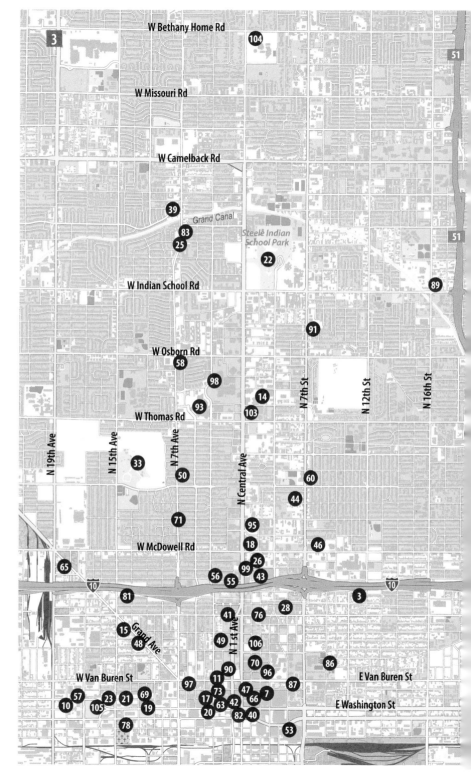

W Bethany Home Rd
104
3
51

W Missouri Rd

W Camelback Rd
51

39
Grand Canal
83
25
Steele Indian School Park
22
89
W Indian School Rd

91

W Osborn Rd
58
98
14
93
103
W Thomas Rd
N 7th St
N 12th St
N 16th St

N 19th Ave
N 15th Ave
33
N 7th Ave
50
60
N Central Ave
44
71
95
W McDowell Rd
18
46
65
26
99
43
10
56 55
81
3
10
41
76
28
15
Grand Ave
49
106
48
86
90
70
97
11
73
96
87
W Van Buren St
47
E Van Buren St
57
23
21 69
17
66 7
10
105
19
63 42
E Washington St
20
82 40
78
53

Travis Swann Taylor
111 Places in Atlanta
That You Must Not Miss
ISBN 978-3-7408-1887-6

Dana DuTerroil, Joni Fincham,
Daniel Jackson
111 Places in Houston
That You Must Not Miss
ISBN 978-3-7408-2265-1

Dana DuTerroil, Joni Fincham,
Sara S. Murphy
111 Places for Kids in Houston
That You Must Not Miss
ISBN 978-3-7408-2267-5

Kelsey Roslin, Nic Yeager,
Jesse Pitzler
111 Places in Austin
That You Must Not Miss
ISBN 978-3-7408-1642-1

Philip D. Armour, Susie Inverso
111 Places in Denver
That You Must Not Miss
ISBN 978-3-7408-1220-1

Cristyle Egitto, Jakob Takos
111 Places in Palm Beach
That You Must Not Miss
ISBN 978-3-7408-2398-6

Laurel Moglen, Julia Posey,
Lyudmila Zotova
111 Places in Los Angeles
That You Must Not Miss
ISBN 978-3-7408-1889-0

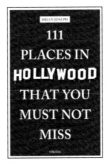

Brian Joseph
111 Places in Hollywood
That You Must Not Miss
ISBN 978-3-7408-1819-7

Floriana Petersen, Steve Werney
111 Places in San Francisco
That You Must Not Miss
ISBN 978-3-7408-2058-9

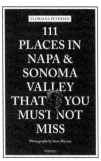

Floriana Petersen, Steve Werney
**111 Places in Napa
and Sonoma That You
Must Not Miss**
ISBN 978-3-7408-1553-0

Floriana Petersen, Steve Werney
**111 Places in Silicon Valley
That You Must Not Miss**
ISBN 978-3-7408-1346-8

Harriet Baskas, Cortney Kelley
**111 Places in Seattle
That You Must Not Miss**
ISBN 978-3-7408-2375-7

Jo-Anne Elikann, Susan Lusk
**111 Places in New York
That You Must Not Miss**
ISBN 978-3-7408-2400-6

Kim Windyka, Heather Kapplow,
Alyssa Wood
**111 Places in Boston
That You Must Not Miss**
ISBN 978-3-7408-2056-5

Brandon Schultz, Lucy Baber
**111 Places in Philadelphia
That You Must Not Miss**
ISBN 978-3-7408-1376-5

Andrea Seiger, John Dean
**111 Places in Washington
That You Must Not Miss**
ISBN 978-3-7408-2399-3

Brian Hayden, Jesse Pitzler
**111 Places in Buffalo
That You Must Not Miss**
ISBN 978-3-7408-2151-7

Amy Bizzarri, Susie Inverso
**111 Places in Chicago
That You Must Not Miss**
ISBN 978-3-7408-1030-6

Photo Credits:

Del Monte Market (ch 27): photo by Rob Wilbanks
Majestic Tempe 7 (ch. 61): photo by Rob Wilbanks
Palm Lane (ch. 71): photo by Rob Wilbanks
Peacock Staircase (ch. 73): Phoenix Convention Center for
    Orpheum Theatre
Redwood Pipeline Scandal (ch. 86): photo by Rob Wilbanks
Uptown Farmers Market (ch. 107): photo by Rob Wilbanks

Art Credits:

9/11 Memorial Pony (ch. 1): Hall of Flame Museum
Airport Art Collection (ch. 2): Aviators, Donald Lipski
Arizona Latino Arts & Cultural Center (ch. 7): *Bird Lady*, Roman
    P. Reyes
Bernie the Robot (ch. 11): Doug Boyd
Flight Goodyear (ch. 36): *Badass*, Randall Hedden
Giant Golden Panda (ch. 43): *Maternal Love*, Gift from City of
    Chengdu to City of Phoenix
Her Secret is Patience (ch. 49): Janet Echelman
Magic Carpet Underpass (ch. 61): *Magic Carpet*, Roberto Behar &
    Rosario Marquardt, R&R STUDIOS
Prince Tribute Mural (ch. 81): Maggie Keane
Rainbow Wings Photo Op (ch. 83): *Rainbow Wings*, Geremy Cites
St. Mary's Basilica (ch. 96): *Pope John Paul II* statue, Roman
    Catholic Church of the Diocese of Phoenix
Sun Worshipper (ch. 98): Holualoa Companies
Susan Arreola Postcard Collection (ch. 99): Phoenix Public
    Library
Tribute to Navajo Code Talkers (ch. 103): Doug Hyde
Water Mark (ch. 107): Laura Haddad & Tom Drugan, commis-
    sioned by Scottsdale Public Art for the City of Scottsdale

Acknowledgements

Most of all, I am grateful for the love, excitement, encouragement, support, and pride in my work from Rob, the reason I came to Phoenix to live this amazing new life. I'm grateful to my friends around the world and my new and dear Phoenix friends Mare, Jeanine, Liz, Heather, and especially Nina, and a special thanks to Justin, Brandon, Jonathan, Olivia, Lupita, and Daisy. Thank you to my brilliant editor and friend Karen Seiger and to Emons Verlag for allowing me to write and photograph this book.

Travis Swann Taylor moved around a lot while growing up throughout the South, Florida, Texas, and even Wyoming. His sense of wanderlust has grown exponentially over the years and continues to take him to exciting and interesting destinations around the world. A self-taught photographer, he has carried a camera since the age of 10. Today, he lives in Phoenix, unexpectedly loving the desert life. He is also the author of *111 Places in Atlanta That You Must Not Miss*.

The information in this book was accurate at the time of publication, but it can change at any time. Please confirm the details for the places you're planning to visit before you head out on your adventures.